THE
ADVENTURES
OF A
BUSH PILOT
II

To, Richards Free Library
Enjoy
Richard Laporte
10/3/2001

RICHARD H. LAPORTE

THE ADVENTURES OF A BUSH PILOT II

Library of Congress Catalogue Number:
2001117396

International Standard Book Number:
0-9658373-1-9

This work is nonfiction
For information address; Richard H. LaPorte
RR 2, Box 128C, Newport, NH 03773

1st printing 2001

CONTENTS

DEDICATION

This book is dedicated especially to those that have chosen their profession as a bush pilot, and to those that have come to realize their dreams getting to own a seaplane to enjoy the thrills of flying north into Canada and Alaska. A way to escape into the wilderness far away from civilization to seek the pleasures of capturing a trophy speckled brook trout, the trophy caribou or moose, or maybe a hectic moment dealing with a grizzly bear.

INTRODUCTION

In my first book titled "The adventures of a bush pilot," I tell about my younger days growing up and becoming a full fledged bush pilot and guide flying mostly in northern Canada and a short time in Alaska by the Bering Sea west of Anchorage.

It is a series of short stories telling all about my flying adventures hunting caribou and moose, dealing with grizzly bears, arctic wolves, and catching some of those hard sought after huge trophy speckled brook trout, arctic char, king salmon, and lake trout. Of course, we also enjoyed fishing for landlocked salmon and many other species of fish.

In this book, "The adventures of a bush pilot II," I will start out by giving step by step procedures for those that wish to become a pilot. Following that, I will walk you through all the necessary information pertinent to safe seaplane flying and becoming a bush pilot. It just may be, that one day some of my little secrets of flying a seaplane may get some pilot out of a jam.

Being that I have an endless amount of adventure stories of my flying as a bush pilot and guide in Canada and Alaska, I hope you will enjoy them. The stories include flying in the Hudson Bay, James Bay area, as well as into Labrador and northern Quebec and Alaska.

INTRODUCTION

I may add, that to me, I do not know of another profession that has given me so much of a challenge and enjoyment. It is such a shame we can't turn the clock back and do it all over again. As the days tick by, I think of all the wonderful years flying in the bush and those hair-raising experiences. It is too bad I couldn't have had all the knowledge I have accumulated when I first started flying, but then, look at all the fun I may have missed.

BECOMING A PILOT

What have I been dreaming about? Is flying a land plane giving me the fun and enjoyment I've been looking for, or should I go for it and get my seaplane rating? Flying is not for everyone, but for those that get the itch to fly, they soon realize "WOW" this is great. Out comes the wallet and a trip to the airport.

You sit down with an instructor and go over the costs of becoming a pilot, at least a private pilot. "Gee", that's only three to five thousand dollars. "Oh", I have to get a flight physical first. That tells me if I am color blind, or my blood pressure is too high or okay. Or my eyesight is good enough to maybe see another airplane crossing my flight path, or can I see good enough to read the chart to show me where I am, or where I am going.

Airport frequencies come in handy to talk to flight control, or flight service. They can help you for dodging air traffic, or tell you which runway to use. Most importantly, you can get some up to date weather information, or get you to where you are going without getting lost and maybe run out of fuel in the process. An "ADF" (Automatic Directional Finder) is great. It shows how far away you are from an airport, if you know the proper frequency. If you are getting low on fuel, at least you can estimate how much time you have left before you crash or make to the airport.

BECOMING A PILOT

Of course, it could be a way of telling you if you are going to be on time, or late for a date to pick up a friend to go flying.

Don't panic, the instructor hopefully will tell you all about this stuff. He or she will get you organized to show you what to do and not to do. By the way, the instructor will tell you to preflight the aircraft you will be flying. Be sure to check the fuel, you don't want to run out of fuel half way across the mountains and have to ditch in the treetops.

Perhaps you should walk around the airplane and check the ailerons and tail section to see if there is any bad cable connections or torn surfaces. Don't forget to check the oil, the engine could seize, making it pretty tuff to fly without that propeller turning. Speaking of propellers, you may want to check the leading edges of the propeller to see how badly worn they are. You may find the engine doesn't run so smoothly if the propeller is out of balance. "Oh," better check the tires, it makes for a tough landing if you happen to blow a tire.

Outside of checking the radio equipment and making sure the instruments and compass are working, the pitot tube attached to the leading edge of the left wing close to the windshield needs to be checked to see if any wasps have packed it with mud.

If that tube isn't open, there will be no free flow of air to the airspeed indicator. Without the use of the airspeed indicator it is difficult to estimate the speed of the airplane for landing or taking off. On the side of the fuselage below the windshield, there is a small hole that feeds static air to some of the instruments. This also has to be free.

BECOMING A PILOT

Now that I have mentioned all this, you need to sit down and absorb what you have just read. Well, to heck with all that, I want to go flying. One way or the other, I am going to get my seaplane rating and maybe become a bush pilot of the north. What ever your goal is, stick with it.

The instructor will more than likely sit down with you and go over a few facts of flying before you take your first flight lesson. You will want to get familiar with the type of aircraft you will be flying. There is a flight manual you should read and get to understand what the particular take-off speed of the aircraft is, what the stall speed is and cruise speed at a given rpm (revolutions per minute of the engine). This is important, as too many rpm's for an extended period of time can damage the engine.

The weight and balance of the aircraft is most important, for if the aircraft isn't loaded properly it can stall on take-off. There is a chart in the manual called the envelope. This tells you where the center of gravity is on the aircraft and the proper load to carry, and where to put it.

You should familiarize yourself with the fuel shut-off valve, usually located on the floor between the front seats. Some fuel shut-off valves control both fuel tanks in one position only. Others, you can select which tank you want to run on. It is always best not to run one tank totally dry. Having a little reserve is very helpful if you happen to run into problems with one tank, pollution, or otherwise.

Once you have taken a few moments to understand some of the important facts of flying and gotten to know a little about the type of aircraft you are about to fly, it is time for you to take your first ride, or lesson. Of course, we expect your instructor will tell you, "lets check the weather before we go."

Who likes to go up on their first flight and have the wind blowing so hard it's hard to control the airplane, or maybe a bunch of thunderstorms are moving into the area. That could cause your hands to get sweated up in a hurry and you feel pressured so much you can't really concentrate on what you are doing.

All of a sudden your clothes feel wet and sticky, and your forehead drips with sweat. You don't need this, so choose a better day when you can get it all together and enjoy your lessons.

I have found that by taking one half-hour sessions lets you take a breather in between lessons, giving one time to absorb things. As one proceeds with more experience, the lessons can be increased in time.

Now that the weather problem has been taken care of, and assuming you have done your preflight on the aircraft, the instructor will walk you out to the aircraft. You will position yourself in the pilot seat (left front seat) and the instructor will sit in the co-pilot seat beside you. He will explain the instruments to you, telling you what they do and their locations.

Checking the radio equipment to see that they are functioning properly and switching to the proper frequency will be one of the first things to do. You certainly don't want to wait until you get into the air and be fumbling around trying to figure what is going on. Someone at the tower or airport may need to contact you, or you them. You don't want to crash on take-off, so you had better reach down and turn the fuel selector valve on.

BECOMING A PILOT

The instructor will tell you to start the engine to warm it up so the engine oil gets up to temperature before take-off. Making sure the engine oil is warm enough will help guard against engine failure. Warm oil helps to lubricate the engine parts a lot better than cold engine oil. Hopefully, the compass at the top of the windshield works, so assuming that's okay, the gyrocompass on the dash should be set accordingly. Tho gyrocompass may have to be reset occasionally while in flight. It is used mainly for coordinated turns or procedural turns that you will learn more about as you continue with your lessons.

Depending on which way the wind is blowing will normally dictate which runway you will be using for take-off. Usually, at small airports there is a windsock indicating the wind direction, "not always dependable," or a call to ground control or someone at the airport can tell you which runway to use. The instructor should get you squared away on that.

Now that all this has been done, you will have to get permission from ground control "if the airport has a tower," to taxi down the taxiway to the proper runway. In the case of a small airport operating with just a unicom service, (122.8) it is usually good practice to notify the airport by radio that you are proceeding to take off from the active runway.

At the end of the runway there should be a warm-up area where a final run-up of the engine is done and checking both magnetos to make sure both are working properly. If a drop of more than one hundred rpm's (revolutions per minute) register on the rpm gauge, it may mean a faulty magneto or spark plugs, or spark plug wires. Both magnetos have to be working properly or the engine will be down on power. You don't need this, you may find it difficult clearing the hills beyond the airport. Be sure to set the altimeter to the altitude of the airport you are at.

A glance into the sky around the airport is necessary in order be on the lookout for other aircraft flying in the vicinity. The last thing you need is to collide with an incoming aircraft as you start your take-off. I hope your instructor will guide you through all this as you go through your stages of learning how to fly.

Well, tighten your seatbelt, it's time to line up the airplane in the center of the runway and shove the throttle in to full position. Keep your feet on the rudder pedals located close to the floor so you can help steer the aircraft straight down the runway.

The rotation of the propeller usually tends to steer the plane to the left so you may have to apply a little pressure on the right rudder.

Having knowledge of the correct airspeed for take-off and one eye on the airspeed indicator will tell you when to pull back on the controls to lift off the runway. You should not pull back abruptly on the controls, but climb out with a shallow climb-out. Otherwise, if you climb too steeply it could cause the airplane to stall, nosing into the runway and crash.

Flying the airplane with a steady hand always brings better and easier flying. Only after a certain amount of experience should a pilot begin to experiment with the airplane. Always treat the airplane and flying conditions with respect. You will live longer.

As you climb up and away from the airport you will look down and find the airport is getting smaller and smaller. At first, the instructor will have you fly what is called (the airport pattern) in order for you to get used to landing and taking off. It's a good idea. You have to land at one point or the other, so you had better practice where it's safe.

Most generally, most approach patterns are one thousand feet above the runway on what is called the downwind part, parallel to the runway. It is best to stay close to the airport when doing your approach in case engine trouble develops.

You then will make a left turn slowing the airplane down by backing off the throttle to lose five hundred feet. Depending on terrain or runway location, an airport may have a right turn approach.

If the airplane engine has a carburetor, you should pull out the carburetor heat lever to help prevent icing of the carburetor. When you turn on final, you should be facing the runway leaving you to drop another five hundred feet before landing.

When coming in for a landing try not to over correct on the controls too much because you may find it causes the airplane to balloon up and down.

It is best to let the airplane sort of do its own thing with a little pressure on the controls as you land and backing off the throttle as needed. Too fast an approach may find you overshooting the runway, so beware of this.

If you have to apply the brakes, pushing on the top of the rudder pedals and pivoting your feet applies the brakes.

Expect to sweat a little on your first few landings, as this is all too new to you unless you have dreamt a lot on how to fly the airplane. So far, so good, you have had a chance to get familiar with the airplane, done a few takeoffs and landings, and of course you have been studying some of the flying books.

Before you solo, you will have to show the instructor you can fly the airplane on your own. You will need to study the weather, cloud formations, rules and regulations on flying, as well as prepare yourself for a few cross-country flights. You will need to know how to map read and what all the different symbols mean.

It is most important to understand the particular frequencies necessary in flying. Different airports may have different control tower frequencies. There are flight service frequencies, VOR stations (visual omni range) for navigating purposes, and airport information frequencies that give you local airport and weather information.

Listed on the flight maps are airline routes, altitudes of mountains and towers, restricted areas, and control zones, as well as the altitudes of some lakes.

Most people just learning to fly will find themselves disorientated when leaving the vicinity of the airport. You could be flying over your own back yard and not recognize where you are. It is quite different looking down from above the ground.

The terrain becomes totally strange to you, especially when flying around the hillsides or mountains. You will find yourself looking at territory you never knew existed. Try to familiarize yourself with hills or lakes.

Rivers make excellent reference points when flying around the countryside. It makes it a lot easier to stay focused as to where you are. Taking a look at your compass every few minutes helps keep you on track as to the direction you want to fly in, but always be on the lookout for other aircraft in the area. Colliding with another aircraft will almost certainly bring you sudden death.

Get yourself a pair of good sunglasses so you won't get blinded when flying directly into the sun, for that might just be the moment when another aircraft may be in front of you. It could also be the case where a high tower may be in your path of flight and blocked out by the sun.

Consulting your flight map of the area you are flying in will help guard against hitting one of these towers. Power lines are a big danger to aircraft. It has happened so many times when even the experienced pilot completely forgets the power lines are there and flies into them.

Most transmission lines are marked on your flight maps, so a careful study of the maps before flying through an area will warn you in advance of the obstacles to be encountered.

You will find that the flight map will be one of the most important items in flying. It gives you a vast amount of information pertaining to flying, such as roads, railroads, altitudes of towers, mountains, some lakes, restricted zones, frequencies of airports and numerous other information.

It is required that a pilot have forty hours of flying time before getting his or hers private pilot's license. A certain amount of dual instrument is required, for if you want to go on and get your commercial license you will need an instrument rating. Knowing how to use the instruments will help keep you out of trouble when going on your first cross-country flight. Most airplanes will have dual navigation radios. When outlining a flight plan before heading out on your first cross-country flight, it is best to have some alternate airports and their frequencies written down in case you encounter bad weather or have an emergency.

VORs (visual omni range) are widely used while navigating in unfamiliar areas. When consulting your flight map you can write down the frequencies of the VOR stations that you can use to fly your cross-country flights.

You can also use the VOR stations off to the right or left of your desired flight path. It will help tell you where you are enroute by setting one of your radios to one of those frequencies and the other radio you will naturally set on the frequency on your scheduled flight path.

When both needles center you can refer to your flight map and that will tell the exact spot where you are. Practice is the best way to overcome any doubts you may have about this method of navigation.

Choosing a safe altitude is also important so as not to fly into a mountaintop, especially when flying in bad weather, or at night.

Taking a ground school will teach you all about these things, but I am sure you will find experience will be the best teacher.

There are many kinds of instructors. Some are easy going and take the time to teach you in such a way that you will not feel you are being under pressure. It may make the world of difference to a beginner. Being new to the flying world, a student finds himself under the gun, so to speak. His brain will be rushing a mile a minute trying to absorb all the things being thrown at him. Don't feel like you have to learn everything in one day like I did. Take your time and get to understand as much as possible. If you have any questions, don't be afraid to ask your instructor or other pilots. Above all, get to know the aircraft you are flying, in every sense. How many gallons per hour the aircraft you are flying consumes is a good start.

Make sure the fuel gauges are working properly. You don't want to be flying on a trip thinking you have plenty of fuel when all the time one of the fuel gauges are reading full when the tank is nearly empty. Always visually check the fuel tanks so you know how much fuel there is. Make sure the engine has plenty of oil. Double-check the magnetos and be sure the engine is running good. Good luck getting your private license. I will see you in the next chapter.

SO YOU WANT TO BECOME A BUSH PILOT

Becoming a bush pilot has been many a pilot's dream. Commercial airline pilots tell me how so many of them envy the life of a bush pilot, how they wish they could have gotten into the profession of a bush pilot and the challenges it gives. In my first book, titled (THE ADVENTURES OF A BUSH PILOT) I tell about how I got started as a bush pilot and some of my wild adventures in northern Canada and Alaska.

There is no doubt about the question, "Gee, is there any excitement in being a bush pilot?" "Is it too dangerous for a regular land plane pilot to jump into?" That is a question only the individual can answer. For myself, I knew in the very beginning that I wanted to become a bush pilot. It was eating at me something terrific, and the only way I was going to satisfy my dreams and desires, was to go and do it.

I must admit, I pushed things a little when I first started out in my episodes of becoming a bush pilot. The same day I finished installing floats on my Cessna 206, I got my seaplane rating, loaded all my survival gear into the seaplane and with only three hours seaplane time, headed eighteen hundred miles north to Hudson Bay in Quebec, Canada. I was one of those guys that thought experience was the best teacher. Of course, I think I had a lot of help from the guy upstairs. He kind of looked over me, helping me

SO YOU WANT TO
BECOME A BUSH PILOT

through my learning stages. Not only that, I believe he gave me the gift to be a bush pilot and to be able to do the things that other pilots found hard to do. I will say one thing, I sure had my fun at it. Sure, there were a few hectic moments, but how else is one to stir up the blood and get the adrenaline flowing. This is what it's all about. If you don't get a thrill out of flying, you may as well hang it up and find some other profession.

Now, it's time to jump into the seaplane and take a ride with me to learn the ropes on bush flying and gain a few bits of the tricks to seaplane flying.

Let's assume that our seaplane is a Cessna 206. This is the type aircraft that I chose to fly twenty plus years as a bush pilot. Other aircraft will vary in performance and handling characteristics, but the basics of seaplane flying are about the same.

Getting to know the type of aircraft you will be flying is very important as to give you a total understanding as to how the aircraft will perform under certain conditions. You don't want to come up with a bunch of surprises in an emergency and be guessing where whatever is and what it does, so let's get down to business and learn a few things about flying a seaplane.

First off, we walk to the dock at the lake and do a preflight on the Cessna 206. We will want to check the floats and pump out any water that may be in the compartments. Keep in mind that occasionally the tubes that run to the bottom of the individual compartments have been known to come loose and prevent pumping the compartments dry. If this happens, it will be necessary to remove the compartment cover and reinstall the tube making sure it is connected to the bottom of the compartment.

We check the fuel drains with a plastic tube kept in the airplane designed for this purpose and proceed to preflight the aircraft as explained earlier in the book. I am going to ride shotgun in the co-pilot seat and the other person who ever it may be, will place himself, or herself in the pilot's seat on the left.

After having done our preflight on the Cessna 206 we untie the rope holding the seaplane to the dock and climb aboard. The next step is to strap our selves in with the seat belts, check the fuel selector valve to make sure it is on, and start the engine.

While we are taxiing warming the engine oil, we review the instruments and radio equipment making sure we have the proper frequency selected to communicate with the local airport, or seaplane base. We shall want to set the altimeter to correspond with the altitude of the lake so as to have a guide as to what altitude you may be landing at, at a later time.

The next step is to do a run-up of the engine to check the magnetos (left and right) by switching the ignition key to the left magneto and then to the right magneto. If the rpm's (revolutions per minute) drop more than one hundred rpm's, it will be a reason to look for problems either in the magnetos, spark plugs, spark plug wires, or another source.

The engine should be revved up to the suggested take-off rpm's for your particular aircraft or within a hundred rpm's to make sure the necessary power will be consistent for take-off and flying.

Assuming things check out okay when doing your run-up of the engine, it is best to follow through with

SO YOU WANT TO
BECOME A BUSH PILOT

your checklist of things to review before take-off. The oil pressure gauge is there for a reason. It is one of the very first things to check visually when first starting the engine. No oil pressure, or low oil pressure means you don't fly the aircraft until it is checked out by a mechanic and the problem fixed.

More accidents have happened through negligence of a pilot. Just because the aircraft was okay the last time it was flown does not mean it will be okay the next time. Being a good pilot does not limit his performance to just flying the aircraft. He has to know everything about his aircraft on the ground, as well as in the air.

On the dash of the Cessna 206, you will find a fuel flow gauge. Here again, it important that you notice the amount of fuel flow indicated when doing your run-up. At the suggested rpm's, the required fuel flow should register on the gauge. If this reads low, there is a problem. It could be a case of a restricted fuel line, dirty filter, or a bad fuel pump.

In some cases that I have run into in northern Canada where I got a bad batch of fuel, mostly water, and the temperature was below freezing. The fuel strainer bowl had frozen solid. On doing my run-up, the fuel flow gauge showed a little low. Some fuel was getting through, but not enough to take off and keep flying.

After further inspection I found the problem to be ice in the fuel bowl. I had to use a warm wet towel to thaw the ice enough to correct the problem. This was a few hundred miles from civilization. Luckily, I was fortunate enough to be able to fix a lot of the problems I encountered throughout my years of being a bush

SO YOU WANT TO
BECOME A BUSH PILOT

pilot. Thank heaven for that. Most all my flying years were spent far from civilization and repair stations.

Supposing I had decided to take off...I may have had enough fuel to take off, but shortly after the engine would have starved for fuel and I would have had no place to go, but down. "Ugly thought..."

Setting the gyro-compass to the magnetic compass before taking off is necessary in case you find yourself having to do procedural turns either in bad weather, or making an approach to an airport.

One last check is to make sure the manifold pressure is reading normal before you take off. With low manifold pressure, the engine will not perform properly. Also, keep in mind not to taxi with the rpm's greater than eight hundred to one thousand. Otherwise, the propeller will pick up too much water and chew away at the leading edge of the propeller.

I guess we have covered enough to get us started, so push the full rich mixture control all the way to the dash and were ready to push the throttle in to build up your speed. Come back on the control to get the nose up as you build the power up to full speed.

The rudders on the floats should be raised for take-off as the rudders are used to help steer the seaplane only while taxiing.

As with the Cessna 206, twenty degrees of flaps are recommended for take-off, so we will want to make sure that is done. It helps get the seaplane onto the step quicker and allows it to lift off sooner. Without using the flaps, a much higher rate of speed will be needed and not recommended.

When the seaplane builds up to a certain speed, the nose of the plane will start to get light so relax the control a little, letting the floats to get on the step. It is called the "step" because on the bottom of the floats toward the rear steps up to a taper to the back of the floats. At this point, you will hold the nose of the seaplane level to the water building your speed to fifty-five to sixty miles per hour (recommended take-off speed for the 206) and pop the plane off the water.

So far, so good... We are going to climb out about eighty to ninety miles an hour and fly around a little while you get familiar with the 206. Getting the feel of the airplane you are flying means a lot in order to do a few procedures well.

First, we will do a few tight turns to the left and to the right keeping the seaplane at the same altitude of about a thousand feet above the lake. Then, we will go up higher and do a few stalls to get the idea how the 206 will react in that situation.

When doing stalls, it is best to back off the power some while raising the nose of the seaplane until the plane drops dramatically off and heads down towards the ground. The idea, is to recover as soon as possible without losing much altitude by increasing the power and bring the nose up and level out.

At all times, be sure to look around you for other aircraft that might be in the area. It could be a crunching blow if you collide with one.

Now, I reach over and shut the engine down and tell you to pick a spot on the lake by a point of land to do a dead stick landing.

Keeping your speed around one hundred miles an hour and checking the direction of the wind, you can show me just how good you are landing into the wind. Bear in mind that winds up to thirty-five miles an hour are okay for a seaplane depending on its size. Much more than that, It becomes a rough situation and a little more dangerous for some pilots. I don't mean to push you being your first time on floats, but why should you be any different than me when I first started out on floats. So... let's get this seaplane up on the step. We are going to do some high-speed step turns to the right, and some to the left.

You will have to be alert and watch that you don't catch a wing tip in the water, I really don't care about taking a swim just now. Step turns are used mainly for getting out of small ponds by circling the perimeter of the pond at high speed on the step, and hopefully, you will be able to get up enough speed to fly out.

It is a good idea to study the wind conditions on the pond before trying to lift off. Mountains or hills surrounding the lakes and ponds can have a devastating effect when it comes to wind conditions.

Being aware of the wind conditions is one of the most important parts of flying a seaplane. The survival rate could be very low for those pilots disregarding the wind factor.

Well, as I say, a little practice makes for a better pilot, but there is nothing like the real thing when you get up north in the real country and get that on the job training. There is something about the North Country, either in Canada, or Alaska, once you cross the border and get a couple of hundred miles north, your whole outlook will be so different. In the case of returning back to the United States border, it is the complete reverse. It's like I want to turn right around and head back north where I feel content and at peace with "Mother Nature."

SO YOU WANT TO
BECOME A BUSH PILOT

I cannot stress the importance of understanding wind conditions and its possibilities of wrecking one's aircraft or life in an instant. Being able to read wind conditions, or directions on a lake can help improve the chances of survival in the North Country.

Hills around a lake or pond may very well dictate as to the direction a pilot wants to land his seaplane. At times, wind can give you false indications on the water due to the way that hills are situated. Many times I have seen where the wind is blowing on the lake in one direction, giving me the idea I should take off against the wind, but found out that I was better off taking off in the opposite direction. The swirling of the winds around the mountains and hills are unpredictable to say the least.

When approaching a lake surrounded by hills, be especially alert for downdrafts. Look for glassy water areas near the base of the hills. This could be an indication of a downdraft. If so, and you feel the seaplane start to drop suddenly, you may find it necessary to push the throttle in for more power to overcome the downdraft. It is always best to have your hand on the throttle when coming in to land in case you need to either back off the power, or to apply power, whichever the case may be.

If you see a glassy water area, which is most likely a downdraft, then you see a rough water area beyond that, there will more than likely be an updraft causing the seaplane to abruptly gain in altitude. There will be an up and down movement of the seaplane that could put the seaplane out of control if you are not quick to respond with the throttle.

Wind conditions are more affected around hills or

SO YOU WANT TO
BECOME A BUSH PILOT

mountains when the wind is out of the southwest causing crosswind conditions. The reason for this, is that most lakes run north and south due the movement of the glaciers years ago. There is usually no problem landing north to south or the opposite when the wind is out of the north or south.

When flying in severe windy conditions, and you need to land, the best thing to do is to seek a quiet cove or sheltered area behind a protected shoreline. A side-hill, or island if necessary, usually gives some protection against the wind. If the wind is gusty, it is best to maintain a higher rate of speed so as to overcome the sudden gusts that can grab the seaplane and flip it. Here again, it is necessary to be ready with your hand on the throttle to help overpower these situations.

When taking off in crosswind conditions with a seaplane, as on wheels, it is safer to lower the wing towards the direction the wind is coming from. This will help guard against the wind from getting under the wing and possibly flipping the aircraft. No one likes bringing up bodies from the bottom of the lake.

A power-off approach is not always the best way to do a landing when in gusty, or windy conditions. After a pilot gets some experience under his belt and he gets to know his aircraft, he will have learned what to do, and not to do, hopefully.

Large bodies of water will produce much larger waves than small bodies of water. Therefore, caution is in order when taking off, or landing on large lakes. The waves can be so huge it is like landing in the middle of the ocean. You may think the aircraft will break in two, or the floats are going to be ripped off.

SO YOU WANT TO
BECOME A BUSH PILOT

The swells are so huge between waves it seems the seaplane is going to get swallowed up. I have seen the waves so big where the seaplane would start to porpoise. It was big trouble. A fairy boat had crossed the Sagenay River in front of me creating huge waves. I had not noticed them until it was too late. My 206 began porpoising so much, I thought I was going to lose it. The only way I could save it, was by holding forward on the controls and diving through the top of the waves until I could get up speed enough to take off. That taught me a lesson. Stay away from fairy boats and their area, landing, or taking off.

Glassy water can be equally as dangerous as rough water, perhaps even more so. Pilots with bad depth perception can experience dreadful situations when trying to land on a pond or lake that is smooth as glass, and shiny like a mirror.

There is no disturbance on the water's surface to tell a pilot how close to the surface he may be. A pilot may think he is a few feet off the water, when in fact he may be five hundred feet above it. He may back off the power to the point of stalling, thinking he is going to touch down on the water right away, but instead, finds himself and the seaplane dropping out of the sky from five hundred feet above, or higher.

Water is as hard as cement in these cases, and usually ends up totally wiping out the seaplane, and taking a few lives in the process.

When landing on glassy water, I find it best to land along the shoreline using the shrubs or trees as a guide. It gives pilots a much easier way of telling how close to the water they are.

A pilot should always be aware when landing on a

SO YOU WANT TO
BECOME A BUSH PILOT

short pond with glassy water. A seaplane will not stop in as short a distance on glassy water as it can when landing into the wind and on a lake with rough water. Therefore, do not expect to pull off a short landing on a small pond that has glassy conditions. You are more apt to find the seaplane sliding on top of the water like you are on ice and smashing into the trees at the end of the pond.

A trick I learned years ago on getting stopped in a short pond has really worked out well for me. Upon landing my seaplane, and as soon as I could level out on the water, I would push forward on the controls causing the front of the floats to dive deep into the water. This acted like a break and would slow the seaplane down in a hurry. I would not suggest this without having some experience under your belt.

If a pilot decides he has to stall the seaplane over the top of the trees at the end of a short pond in order to get stopped before hitting the trees at the other end, he may find himself in a bit of a predicament. Pilots have to take into consideration the possibility of not getting the seaplane out without the help of a helicopter.

It is quite possible to land a seaplane in a shorter distance than what you need to take off. That would be very embarrassing when you are several hundred miles from civilization.

I have always considered a seaplane to give a pilot a little more leeway safety-wise, as opposed to a land plane. Especially flying in the North Country where there are few or no roads. A land plane would have a tough time landing in a swamp, compared to a seaplane.

SO YOU WANT TO
BECOME A BUSH PILOT

If worse came to worse, and a pilot had to set the seaplane into the trees, the floats would act as a cushion, where the aircraft on wheels would not have that luxury. I have found the floats to work well when landing on snow or ice when it is necessary. Though this may not be a standard practice, and not to be done without checking the landing area, it serves its purpose, thus making the seaplane quite versatile.

Now that I have strayed away from our first few lessons of getting to know what its like to fly a seaplane, I felt it was necessary to educate you in all aspects of the different kinds of problems a seaplane pilot may encounter. I didn't have anyone to tell me all these things before I headed to the North Country and Alaska. I had to learn it the hard way, but I sure did enjoy every bit of it.

It would be difficult for an instructor to put you through all of the things I have told you about. He can put you through the beginning stages of becoming a seaplane pilot, but the rest would have to be up to you.

Flying a seaplane is one thing, but a pilot also has to be able to dock his seaplane safely without wrecking the floats or airplane. This is where understanding wind conditions are very important. The wind can grab the tail section of the seaplane making it difficult to steer it to a dock or particular spot on shore, and avoiding rocks or trees. You will have to learn how to judge the wind to make your proper approach.

Another important concern, at one time or the other it will be necessary to step onto the floats with the engine still running. The propeller has been known to cut heads or arms off when the person on the floats gets careless and forgets about getting too close to the propeller. It is just a very bad move to step forward on the floats when the engine is running. So I strongly suggest you shut the engine off, and the magnetos, unless you absolutely need it running.

It is a very good idea to double-check the ignition switch to make sure both magnetos are off before exiting the cockpit. Some seaplanes are equipped with a cable stretching between the front of each float making it handy to get to one side of the seaplane or the other. People have been known to walk across the cable and grab the propeller to catch their balance. The slightest movement of the propeller can start the engine when the magnetos are on, causing an ugly scene.

Always show caution when walking around your aircraft. Never trust the other person when giving him instructions, you will live longer. You are the pilot, the captain of your ship, so it is up to you to make sure that everything is okay.

Now that you have listened to me about all the things you should and shouldn't do, and you managed to get your seaplane rating, we will head north and get some real on the job training.

FLYING NORTH

The long awaited day has come. We have loaded the seaplane with all of the essential equipment for survival. Such as sleeping bags, extra fuel, tent, axe, fishing gear, matches in a dry container, and plenty of food to last a few days beyond our expected return date in case of bad weather, or whatever may arise.

We also must make sure we have the necessary maps of the area we are to fly, and above all, know where to get fuel in the North Country.

The availability of fuel can be a big problem up north. A pilot should become familiar with the whereabouts of seaplane bases. That is why I have always found it better to go prepared with extra fuel and engine oil on board in case you over extend your flying because of bad weather, or you are just wanting to get to that last fishing hole for the day.

Throughout the many years that I have flown as a bush pilot and guide, about everything you ever could have imagined has happened to me, but I am still here wanting to go back for more. I guess once this kind of flying gets in your blood, it's hard to quit.

Now that the seaplane is loaded with all the necessary gear, the last minute check of the weather is very important. Our flight will originate from Lake Sunapee, New Hampshire, and our destination will be the headwaters of the Caniapiscau River in northern Quebec. I usually make this trip by going the way of two choices.

The first choice is to fly from Lake Sunapee in a northerly direction until we pick up the Connecticut River north of Hanover. Follow the river north and then on to the Canadian border by Newport, Vermont where we can clear Canadian Customs at a dock on the west shore of Lake Memphremagog. This leg of the trip is about one hour and fifteen minutes.

Our next leg will take us in a northeasterly direction past Sherbrooke, Canada and on to the St. Lawrence River just east of Quebec City. We will follow the St. Lawrence River all the way to Baie Comeau and land at a seaplane base about a mile up the Manicouagan River north of the St. Lawrence River.

There are quite a few power lines in the area so caution should be used. Also, there are several dams in the vicinity and one should be alert for pulpwood in parts of the Manicouagan River. It is about a two hour and forty-five minute flight from Lake Memphremagog to Baie Comeau with a Cessna 206.

Flying this route provides a margin of safety by being over water most of the trip. I usually prefer to make my flights over water whenever possible even if it requires longer flight time. Just a little extra caution in case something goes wrong. Never totally trust the mechanic that worked on your aircraft.

Baie Comeau airport has a tower, and the guy working it usually is on the ball taking special notice of any aircraft coming and going, even at the seaplane base. They like to show their authority and want to know where you are going and where you just came from. Of course, it is nice if you have filed a flight plan.

FLYING NORTH

That makes them happy. Sometimes it gripes me when I have to file a flight plan, good or bad. Because when I am flying in bad weather conditions I never know when I have to set down. It is almost impossible when flying at low altitudes to make contact with an airport unless you are in their back yard. The next thing that happens, if you can't make contact to close your flight plan, and your setting on some lake back in the boonies, an alert goes out. They put you on the missing list and all heck breaks loose.

I might add, that flying the St. Lawrence River provides a person with some enjoyable sights. For those that like to enjoy whale watching, this certainly is the way to go. The huge black whales rising to the surface and shooting their big spouts of water is quite a sight in itself while watching their enormous tail strike the water.

Flying low over the St. Lawrence River has always been a very interesting flight. When we have flown level to the decks of some of the freighters transporting cargo, we get a chance to look over the crew and wave to them. I guess they get a kick out of that.

As we fly along the St. Lawrence River we encounter many seals along the sandbars, ducks and geese, along with many white whales, especially in the area of the Sagenay River. If you want to have a hair-rising experience, try landing or taking off in the fog on the St. Lawrence River and have a huge black whale surface right in front of the seaplane. Better yet, try taxiing through the thick fog and end up getting stuck on a sandbar. This is what I love about seaplane flying. Always something new happening. What a thrill!

Well, we have refueled at Baie Comeau and ready to head north. Our pockets are a little lighter as gas in

FLYING NORTH

Canada is expensive, but that's okay, we are going to have a good time. This last leg of the trip is approximately one and one half-hour in duration bringing us to the headwaters of the Caniapiscau River. We will have flown north following the Manicouagan River for at least one hour to the Manicouagan Reservoir created by a meteorite years ago. This is a huge circular body of water with a large island in the middle. It also happens to be an area where a line is drawn for encountering bad weather and fog.

The Manicouagan Reservoir is well known for its fishing for salmon, brook trout, northern pike, and lake trout. Every pilot with a seaplane or operator of a boat that chooses to land on this body of water should be aware of the huge waves that can come up in minutes when the wind decides to kick up a storm. It can be very treacherous and most dangerous. Talk about landing in the ocean, try this one on for size.

Flying north of the Manicouagan Reservoir we will follow another river, and over hundreds of lakes of all shapes and sizes. Many of the lakes are shallow and very rocky and will not provide you with a safe place to land the seaplane. Most of the large lakes in the North Country contain many rocks and rocky reefs just under the surface.

An experienced bush pilot will not land on any body of water without checking it out by first flying over the area he wants to land. The cost of repairing a damaged aircraft in the North Country is prohibitive and I cannot stress the importance of using caution at all times. Many airplanes have been wrecked and laying around the North Country and donated to the Queen of England, being that she owns northern Canada. What usually happens after a crash, the vultures of the north (guys working in the North Country), sea-plane bases or etceteras swoop in and rob what they can of whatever is salvageable.

Extra caution is required when landing in rivers due to currents and the way rocks are moved about from the spring breakup of ice. I have found that rivers have changed quite a bit from one year to another. One should never take for granted that because it was safe to land in a particular part of a river last year does not mean it is okay this year. It goes back to the old business of always flying over the area you want to land in if you want to survive as a bush pilot.

One important factor to consider when landing on narrow bodies of water such as rivers or narrow lakes is the wind conditions. There are certain times when a pilot will choose not to land in some lakes or rivers because of crosswinds.

Many pilots find themselves in deep trouble trying to overcome crosswinds that usually cause severe updrafts and downdrafts. Hills or trees lined along the rivers can raise havoc deflecting the wind in all direc-tions. I have always thought it was safer to approach a landing at higher speeds when confronting cross-wind conditions. When landing at a slower speed the wind has more of a tendency to have more affect on the airplane.

Flying close to the water's surface does not give a pilot the freedom of space and maneuverability as apposed to flying a few hundred feet off the water. You are limited considerably when recovering from a near accident in these situations that could result in death and the loss of your aircraft.

Now that we have a better understanding of flying a seaplane and the things to look out for, we can set up camp and get down to the reason for flying north, "fishing." We had lucked out weather-wise flying the whole trip from New Hampshire to northern Quebec. This is not a normal thing to happen, as in the past, I have had to fly through three or four different weather systems making the difference of really enjoying the trip, or busting my back battling the rain, snow, fog, or big winds.

Though I prefer an overcast day to fly and not have that bright light in my eyes called the sun, when there is clouds, it usually means bad weather lurking in the shadows. I always tell the people flying with me, "when we see a line of clouds on the horizon ahead of us, within a half hour or forty-five minutes we will be right in the middle of bad weather."

When flying in the North Country it is a good idea to keep your eyes on the outside temperature when the weather is bad. It can dictate as to how your flight goes. Any time the temperature gets in the thirties and it is raining, there is a good possibility of icing conditions. The leading edges of the wings can ice up causing the airplane to fly sluggish and possibly to stall out of the sky if it gets too excessive. The temperature gauge can give you some warning of this happening, so be aware of temperature changes.

Too much heavy wet snow can really be a danger. It can build up at a rapid pace on the wings and struts and the first thing you notice, "gee this airplane is not flying so well." The airplane suddenly has gotten so much heavier and just does not respond to the controls very well. "What do I do now?" Stick my head out the window to see where I am going, or maybe it's best to drop altitude to see if the difference in the temperature will melt the snow. If not, the next best thing would be to land the airplane and wash off the surfaces and wait for the weather to break.

Water from a lake works real well. This is another good reason for carrying a bucket in the airplane as part of your gear besides using it for carrying water to put out a camp fire, or transfer gas from a drum to the wing tanks.

Now that we have established our base camp at one of my secret fishing spots and sorted our gear for the following day of fishing, we can review some of the important points I have been explaining about flying up north. A good hot meal cooked over an open fire is in order, and a good night's rest will put us in good shape for an early morning rise.

Perhaps I am getting ahead of myself when I expect a pilot green behind the ears and wanting to learn the ropes of becoming a bush pilot to think he can relax. Can you imagine all the things going on in that brain of his? With all the thoughts of being able to catch some of those huge trophy brook trout and salmon along with all that I have told him about flying, I can only relate to when I first flew to Hudson Bay with only three hours seaplane time under my belt.

Come morning, I had no problem getting the gang out of the sack. They were already up and had a roaring fire going with the smell of bacon and eggs. From past experience I was well aware how gung-ho the guys were on the first couple of days. They just couldn't wait to wet their lines in the rapids and hook onto one of those trophy trout.

It seemed they had a lot of questions over breakfast. "Where are we going?" "Do I think the weather is going to be okay?" "Are the fish going to bite today?" "What happens if we fly out and the weather turns bad and we can't make it back to camp?" The answer to all these questions is, "we don't fly anywhere unless we take our sleeping bags and survival gear with us."

As it turned out, it was decided we would spend the first day exploring the fishing near camp. We should take notice of how much fuel we have on board, plus the extra fuel in cans before we go flying off somewhere. The nearest seaplane base to refuel would be at Labrador City and we must make sure we save enough fuel with some to spare to get there.

This is one of the biggest concerns about flying around the North Country. Places to refuel the seaplane are far and few between. Running out of fuel is the last thing a pilot wants to do.

It is many a sportsman's dream to be able to fly back where few people go and set up camp next to one of the best fishing rivers in the north. Imagine a few rolling hills with scattered spruce trees, and the ground is covered with one great blanket of moss. Caribou trails wind their way through the countryside providing footpaths for those that want to take a hike over the hills.

Walking to the top of a nearby hill you can gaze across miles and miles of scattered lakes and rivers clean to the horizon. Throughout the hills the occasional caribou can be seen grazing on the moss called "lichen" while waiting for the big herds to meet up with them to make their way to northwestern Quebec. During the months of August and September is when the caribou start their long migration journey from eastern Quebec and Labrador.

With waders on, and fishing rods in hand, we walk to the river's edge studying the current looking for that special place to cast. The shadow of a trophy brook trout is seen darting through the water as it makes its way around the boulders searching for a quiet place to rest.

Just behind a large boulder protruding from the water was a small area protected from the rushing water dashing on either side of the boulder. From past experience, it tells me these are the places one can expect to catch a beautiful brook trout. No sooner had those thoughts come to mind when a trophy brook trout came leaping out of the river and take a fly that dare play too close to the surface of the water.

It didn't take long for the adrenaline to kick in and a surge of blood rush to our heads. The fishing fever had its grip on us and the long flight north was behind us. Now it's time for some real fun.

LEARNING TO FLY AND FISH IN NORTHERN QUEBEC

Learning to fly in civilization is one thing, but flying in northern Quebec or Canada is something a pilot can find quite different. It seems the further north one flies, the more drastic the weather changes. Never take for granted the beautiful blue sky, for in a matter of a few moments a sudden storm with all its ferocity can sweep in on you creating havoc. The North Country is to be respected totally if one wishes to survive as a bush pilot.

As you're flying along under a few scattered fair weather clouds the weather may be beautiful, but ahead of you is a huge mushroom looking cloud. The closer you get to the cloud, you all of a sudden become aware of the darkness of the water of the lakes below.

The lakes behind you were calm and peaceful, but now, strong winds are kicking up some huge waves and enormous wind gusts are streaking across the surface of the lakes.

Something tells you, you are beginning to feel the wrath of that big mushroom cloud. You ask yourself, "what is going on? How come it was so nice flying before, and now it has gotten so rough?" What pilots may not realize, especially those that do not have experience in the North Country, these mushroom clouds are huge storm factories. Everything from large balls of hail, to powerful winds and rain are thrown out from these clouds making it a very dangerous situation.

LEARNING TO FLY AND
FISH IN NORTHERN QUEBEC

If you want to live, it is best to give these mushroom clouds a wide birth. Perhaps even better, when caught up in one these situations, head for the nearest sheltered area on a lake and ride it out. These clouds are very fast moving and you can be on your safe way in a matter of moments.

Keeping in mind, winds above thirty-five miles an hour are not considered safe for a seaplane. How much can you or your seaplane handle, if you get caught up in a sudden storm? These are questions you have to ask yourself if you want to play on the edge, pushing things to the extreme.

Thunderstorms are more dangerous due to lightning. Wind, hailstones, and rain accompany most thunderstorms. Thunderstorms are known to go many thousands of feet up and way beyond the altitude a small airplane not equipped with oxygen can fly.

Some pilots have made the wrong decision to try and fly above these storms and find themselves in deep trouble. The best thing is to avoid these kinds of storms. Give them a wide birth.

During the summer months one would expect to have nice weather, warm temperatures with no fear of snowstorms. But in the North Country, never put your trust in what should be. There have been many times over my years as a bush pilot during July and August I have encountered many snowstorms. That is why I insist, when we fly out from our base camp we make sure we take our survival gear with us. Items such as tents, sleeping bags, extra food and fishing rods, as well as a frying pan.

One of the main concerns when flying to remote rivers or lakes to go fishing, a pilot should remember

LEARNING TO FLY AND
FISH IN NORTHERN QUEBEC

to check his supply of fuel. There are times when too much excitement causes a person to be somewhat careless and forgets to go through his checklist. Above all, a pilot has to save enough fuel to get him to a seaplane base. An airplane doesn't run too well without fuel and it is almost impossible to think a person can walk out of the North Country.

There are literally thousands of lakes and rivers in northern Quebec and Labrador that a person would have to cross to get to some sort of civilization. In most cases the water temperature would be too cold and unbearable to swim a great distance. Especially when the end of August approaches and the cold nights lower the water temperature in a hurry.

Some of the sportsmen that I have taken up north think they want to take a refreshing swim, but find it quite a surprise when their body strikes the water. With a big "shriek" they are out of there in a hurry, saying, "that's enough for me."

Now that we have reviewed some of the things we are supposed to do and not to do to keep us out of trouble for a while, we can go back to that river where we saw all those nice brook trout swimming around.

There is a science to fishing a river, and the best way I know how to learn all this is to fish with a guide that has fished the rivers. Brook trout in particular spook very easy. It is best not to make much movement when casting, working the different areas of a river. Time, and time again, when we have located a hotspot for fishing and the guys get so excited catching trout, they start running all over the place and their movement spooks the trout. Either that, or because they have caught so many trout out of one area it spooks the trout. When the brook trout shut down we have no other choice but to jump in the seaplane or boat and head for another spot.

Flying over northern Canada takes you over some of the most beautiful territory. I can only describe it as something out of a different planet. Caribou trails crisscross hundreds of miles of rolling hills covered with moss and wild blueberry bushes. It is hard to distinguish the many caribou that lay among the hills because they blend in so well with the moss.

Depending on how late in the summer the temperature stays warm dictates as to when the caribou start their migration. Usually, the months of August and September is the prime time for caribou hunting. Preferably, September is the better time for hunting because by this time the big trophy bulls have shed their velvet exposing a beautiful set of antlers with their shiny varnished surface. The female caribou have antlers as well, but they are much smaller with several prongs. They do not have the double shovels on the front of their antlers like so many of the bulls do.

Flying above the fifty-third parallel, we find ourselves looking at thousands of lakes and rivers that stretch far beyond the horizon. Black spruce stunted from the severe winters and short summers occasionally dot the shorelines of the many lakes and rivers. A four inch black spruce tree shows on its growing rings when a tree is cut through tells the long life of this small tree as to being about one hundred and thirty-seven years old. Depending on what part of the North Country you are at, finding firewood could be a big problem.

LEARNING TO FLY AND
FISH IN NORTHERN QUEBEC

When flying along the sixty-ninth longitude and starting at approximately the fifty-second parallel the rivers run north and south. It seems like you are at the top of the world. Where the rivers run east you can find yourself in Labrador and where the rivers run west you will be in Quebec. Below the fifty-third parallel one can expect to see a much more wooded territory, as opposed to above the fifty-third parallel.

From years of flying in the North Country I have gained the knowledge of being able to pick out the better fishing spots for the trophy speckled brook trout. A Canadian sectional flight chart of eight miles to the inch gives good detail.

Picking out a set of rapids on a river running between two large lakes is what I like to look for. A few deep holes make ideal places for the brook trout to hang out. Sections where the river makes a bend providing a backwater and a few large boulders for the trout to lurk behind are also good places to fish.

Don't discount the heads of the rapids where the river flows out of the large lakes. There have been many times when I have landed on such lakes and taxied the seaplane close to the mouth of the river, got out the fishing rod and "bam" a huge brook trout would leap into the air striking at the fly.

Working the slick current from the further shore to where I would be standing, I would cast a fly or lure letting it do its thing as I retrieved my line. Huge brook trout and salmon were laying there waiting for some sort of bait to drift down the river ready to strike.

Huge northern pike lurking in the shadows of the slower water would be ready for the first small trout to stray out of the fast water. We found the size of the

LEARNING TO FLY AND
FISH IN NORTHERN QUEBEC

trout to be absolutely amazing and we were catching lake trout up to forty-three pounds struggling against the rapids feeding on whatever they could grab. It certainly is quite a contrast compared to our fishing here in New Hampshire.

It is quite common to catch a large brook trout in the five to nine pound range with several mice in their stomach. So what do we do, We put an imitation mouse on our fly line, cast it out, and "wow" a big old brook trout comes flashing out of the water with that imitation mouse in its jaw. I must say, it is quite a thrill landing one of those trophy brook trout.

They dive from one end of the rapids to the other, and when they get into one of the deep holes the first thing they want to do is rap them selves around a large boulder. One has to be careful about the line being cut on the sharp rocks. The trout seem to know what they are doing to cut the line and the next thing you know the trout is running free as a breeze down the river with half of your line.

Flies such as the muddler minnow, red and white streamers, mickey finns, and an assortment of other flies popular for brook trout work well in the North Country. When fishing the rivers, it is best to study the currents and channels. Some of the deeper channels in the rivers can provide excellent fishing.

Knowing how to fish the proper spots will produce some fantastic results. It is better not to disturb the waters any more than necessary, but of course when you hook onto one the those huge trout a person doesn't have much choice. By the time the big trout get through thrashing around trying to throw the hook, they shake up the rest of the trout in the area. That is why it is best letting the trout run easy with just a little strain on the line and working the trout in slowly, instead of trying to haul it in, in a hurry.

Walking on rocks covered with moss can be most dangerous. As much as I have run up and down the rivers up north I still manage to take a header and end up sitting in the river up to my neck in water. With the chilly waters, I could only gasp for breath while I scrambled out of the water in a hurry.

Hip boots having felt soles are a big help. It allows one to walk across the slippery rocks with more ease without slipping. One guy says, "what good are hip boots if you're going to fall into the water anyway, you are going to wind up wet?" The boots will also help protect your ankles while walking around the rocks. Not only that, but if you get stuck in the mud, you can yank your feet out of the boots, then pull the boots out of the mud with your hands.

Conditions are worse at the beginning of the season when the frost hasn't totally worked its way out of the edge of the rivers. Certain times when the pressure is low and stormy weather hangs around for a few days the trout have been known to shut down. It's like they don't want to eat, it doesn't matter what kind of fly or lure you use, they just won't bite.

When fishing gets that bad, I have a secret weapon. I take a piece of fish and put it on my hook with a little weight and let it sink to the bottom of the big holes. This usually will bring great results. The big "lunkers" resting at the bottom of the holes will take that when they won't take anything else. I often ask myself, "what kind of fishing trip would I have without a seaplane at my disposal?"

LEARNING TO FLY AND
FISH IN NORTHERN QUEBEC

Being able to jump into the seaplane to fly off to some remote lake or river certainly has its advantages. For whatever reasons, if the fishing happens to be poor in one area, I was always lucky to be able to fly my friends to better fishing spots. That's because I knew so much about the North Country.

Just imagine landing the seaplane on a remote lake and pulling up to the mouth of the rapids. As we gaze around studying the river and its potential places to fish, the thought comes over our mind. "What huge trophy brook trout there must be waiting for that first fly to be cast into the water?" "The big male trout in the middle of their spawning season with their red bellies and beautiful red, blue, and purple spots on their sides." The old warriors with their hooked jaw that have never laid eyes on a man standing beside the stream with his fishing rod poised to cast that fly.

How many a fisherman's dream to be with me on one of these fishing trips so far up north. If they only knew about the secret fishing holes that I hold such fond memories of. I tell people, "it's a mistake for us not to catch a fish almost every cast or so."

The big thing is, one never knows what he is apt to hook onto. It could be a huge northern pike up to five feet long, a big lake trout, possibly even a muskellunge, or a world record size speckled brook trout.

It was late August one year when we decided to fly north of my camps to explore some areas for new fishing spots. The weather was a bit "iffy". Rain, snow, and fog shrouded the hillsides making us wonder if it was worth flying out. The thought of sleeping in the bush in a tent with all the foul weather wasn't exactly appealing to us, but what the heck, we really didn't

LEARNING TO FLY AND
FISH IN NORTHERN CANADA

fly all this way to the North Country to sit around the camp to play cards.

There was a place about thirty minutes flying time north of the camp, if we could just make it there we could perhaps get into some good fishing for brook trout. With the weather being bad, along with the sudden changes in temperature gave me some concern, but the yearn to go fishing was just too great.

Making sure we had our survival gear on board, everyone climbed into the 206 Cessna and off we go, due north. For a few minutes the flying was great, but soon, we found ourselves smack dab in the middle of a big snow squall. Visibility was down to nothing and the only way was to fly at tree top level and water level.

At times, I had to keep tipping the wings of the airplane to allow me to see how close my floats were to the top of the trees. Every time we came to the smallest of hills, it became a struggle to avoid them and still be able to map read.

Wherever there was a body of water, it was like I had to call on every bit of experience I had to try and distinguish if it was the same body of water I was looking at on my flight map.

The place we wanted to fish could be over-flown or bypassed very easily because of being so small and the poor visibility hiding it from my view. It was like dodging in and out of the snow squalls hoping we could hit the right spot when the visibility was best. Once we were in the storm it didn't make much sense to turn around and try to make it back to camp being so early in the day. In the North Country snow squalls come and go all day long when the right temperature and wind direction exist. A bush pilot learns to fly in these conditions and just hopes he makes the right decisions.

Many times a pilot is fooled by what we call sucker holes. This is when an opening in the clouds appears, and you may even see the sun shining down through. Your passengers will get all excited and say "wow, the weather is clearing, let's go, or let's head for that opening." In a matter of minutes these so-called sucker holes can close in, trapping you in the clouds or storm and leave you no where to go but into a hill.

A pilot is stupid to fly blind through the clouds in the North Country when he is on floats and doesn't have any instruments to tune in on to take him to safety. Imagine trying to make an instrument approach on a lake nestled among the hills during a storm with no instrument approach system.

My theory in bush flying is, "I don't care how low I have to fly as long as I can see where I am going." That is, as long as I miss the tree tops.

Well, it's a good thing I have a good sense of direction and my airplane follows my touch on the controls. Right in front of our noses lay below us the fishing spot we had set out for. It was a small lake between two stretches of river, large enough to take off with the seaplane. The river flowing out of the lake had several beautiful sets of rapids and deep holes providing just the right ingredients for some fantastic fishing.

It is always most important to find a suitable and safe place to park the seaplane out of harms way of rocks especially if the wind comes up. The aluminum floats are easily damaged when rubbed against rocks.

LEARNING TO FLY AND
FISH IN NORTHERN QUEBEC

A lot of times, rocks rub against rivets causing them to be loose, It is amazing how much water can leak by one loose rivet, filling a compartment in the floats in a matter of minutes or hours. That is why we should make sure we check the floats for water by pumping each individual compartment. Too much water in the floats can prevent the seaplane from taking off, or in cases where a short take-off is required, a pilot may find himself in deep trouble trying to clear the trees at the end of the lake or pond.

After securing the seaplane to the shore next to the mouth of the river, my friends and I made our way down the river studying the rapids and channels for the best likeable fishing spots.

To our nice surprise, sunshine had poked its way through the clouds warming the air, bringing more delight to our fishing. Wherever a fly was cast, there seem to be a huge trophy speckled brook trout waiting among the rocks in the river. Trout after trout rose to the surface, leaping into the air trying to throw the hook that hung in its jaw.

The flexibility of my friend's "Orvis" fly rod time and time again did its job in landing five to ten pound brook trout. A selection of several rods of different weights added to the fun and thrills of fishing for one of the most sought after species of fish in the north. Mother Nature had done her job in painting the speckled brook trout so beautifully. All we can say is "let's put this beautiful trout back in the water so perhaps someone else may enjoy the experience of catching one of these beauties. It may even be, that some "Dad" may bring his son to the North Country to enjoy one of "Mother Nature's" wonders.

LEARNING TO FLY AND
FISH IN NORTHER QUEBEC

Working our way down stream to a bend in the river we came upon a beautiful deep hole loaded with eight to ten pound brook trout. What a sight to see! "Such huge trout and so many to be in one hole." With each cast a trout would rush to the surface grabbing the fly ready for its taking. A large swirl appeared in the water indicating the size of the fish and the battle was on, and so was the excitement. From one end of the pool to the other the trout ran, diving deep into the river hoping to cut the line on the many rocks that lay on the bottom and swim to its freedom. At times, in its violent struggle to free itself, it would leap out of the water to the open space of air shaking its head from side to side, but only to fall victim to a waiting net.

If a person could only picture himself standing on a large boulder on the edge of the river looking down into the deep hole and seeing such beautiful trophy trout swimming around like we have experienced, it would be a life time dream. As I write this story, I think back of the many such fishing trips and the hundreds of photos in my album that I share with so many. I relive my many memories by doing slide and talk shows for many groups and organizations.

With a "well balanced" fly rod like the "Orvis" my friends that have flown north with me have enjoyed their fishing trips tremendously. This particular watershed, all part of the great Caniapiscau River is well known for its salmon "known as ounaniche" and speckled brook trout fishing. Many huge lake trout and northern pike have also been caught in these waters. Because of our love for the enjoyment catching these beautiful fish, for the most part, we have a catch and release policy.

LEARNING TO FLY AND
FISH IN NORTHERN QUEBEC

We decided to head down river to slower water and investigate some northern pike fishing. Our success with brook trout fishing called for a change in menu. Well it didn't take long. A few casts with a big daredevil and all heck broke loose. Just around the corner from where we were catching the brook trout was a small backwater. Backwaters are normally described as a calm body of water, but on this day, it was far from calm.

In a matter of moments there was an explosion of great magnitude. An enormous northern pike had struck our lure with such fury, that calm body of water became alive with a vicious thrashing of a fish fighting for its life to get free. It was like we had hooked onto a shark, but this guy meant business. No way were we going to land this fish without a struggle.

One of my friends was yelling, "grab a club." Another was yelling, "I'll get him, bring it over close to me." One has to be careful not to get his hand cut with the sharp teeth of a pike, let alone his gills. The pike raced from one end of the pool to the other before it tired and we were able to land it. It is possible to squeeze the eyeballs of a pike to paralyze it while handling it in order to get the hook out of its jaw. One northern pike after another were caught, bringing to a close a great day of fishing.

Several hours of fantastic fishing gave us a very satisfying experience. We could not have asked for better fishing, but as the day wore on, the weather began to deteriorate. The threat of more snow was telling us it was time to head back for camp. We did not relish the thought of camping out in miserable weather, and the longer we procrastinated, the less chance we had of getting back to camp.

We could not help but think how lucky we were to have hit the peak spawning period of the speckled brook trout. Being so far north, the trout spawn much earlier than the trout down south due to the difference in temperature and climate. Usually, the month of August is when the trout spawn in the north with the middle of the month being the prime time.

The spawning period may be set back slightly when an exceptionally warm summer has occurred. By the 1st of September the water has cooled off and the trout are through their spawning. Most will have left the rivers and headed for the deep holes in the lakes where they will stay until the next spawning season.

Happy with having such a good day of fishing, it was time to think about heading back to camp. I knew if we pushed the time limit of getting out of here, we might find ourselves fighting snow squalls on the way back and sitting on some lake spending the night. It wasn't very difficult to convince my friends to load their gear into the seaplane to head south, but first we had to get out the bucket brigade and dip water from the lake to wash off the snow and ice from the wings and floats.

Climbing upon the slippery wings is kind of treacherous, for one small slip and I could find myself falling into the icy water of the lake, or bouncing my head off one of the floats. Being hundreds of miles from civilization how many chances does a pilot want to take. Having too much snow and ice on the aircraft can hinder take-off performance creating a situation where a pilot may find the trees at the end of the lake sticking up a little too high. You're either going to crash, or you may pick up a few tree samples. If you're lucky, you just might make it out of there safely. Usually, the guys with you don't really understand how close things get at times. But hopefully, they get a kick out of flying, and say, "well, we got lucky and made that one."

This is a case where the pilot has to know his limits and the aircraft he is flying. Never forget that word "respect" for your flying and the people you fly. Some pilots are too "Gung Ho" and think, "Oh heck, I can make it, I've done this plenty of times." It doesn't always work that way. Old "Mother Nature" can show her wrath at times when she wants to and nobody can change that.

As expected, it was touch and go with snow squalls on the way back to camp, requiring some treetop and water level flying, but this time luck was on our side, arriving back at camp before darkness overtook us.

I don't really have an answer to why I enjoy the challenges of the North Country so much, except I seem to have that wild spirit born in me. My life seems so empty without having something to do to stir my blood, or is it that a little adventure helps fill my void.

One good thing about being back at camp, we have a chance to relax and talk about the day's events. Of course, that is over a good home cooked meal of trout and home fries with a side dish of vegetables.

A few games of darts to top the day off and swapping of stories and maybe a little card game or two usually would wind up in discussions of the next day's plans. How could anyone expect to top today's fishing with the exception of a few snowstorms to cope with.

LEARNING TO FLY AND
FISH IN NORTHERN QUEBEC

As each day passed, it was normal for the sports to sleep in later and later. Everyone is so anxious to go fishing when we first arrive at camp, but after two or three days of hard fishing, and very successful I might add, they seem to want to lay around and take it easy. It takes the pressure off of me when this happens, but I had some new adventure in store for them.

The talk of catching arctic char got the boys stirred up, so I got out the flight maps that would lead us two to three hundred miles north east of Schefferville. Not knowing where or what part of the North Country I am apt to fly, I always carry my brief case full of maps.

Schefferville is one of the last jumping off places in northeastern Quebec for fishing and caribou hunting. We usually refuel at a seaplane base located on a large lake at the north end of town. Schefferville was noted for its mining of iron oar, but when the mines shut down it became a ghost town so to speak. It also has an airstrip for commercial airlines that fly in the sportsmen from the United States and south.

Most of the housing units owned by the mining companies were sold for the mere sum of one dollar, leaving the new owners to pay the property taxes. Since, the mining companies have tried to repurchase the homes. Most of the Cree Indians that lived in the area were moved to a reservation southeast of Schefferville, but this turned out to be very unsatisfactory with the Crees.

My friends were excited to leave the camp for a new fishing adventure. Making sure that all of our survival gear and extra food was on board the seaplane, our first stop would be at Schefferville to refuel. This was a must, because of the lack of seaplane bases in the north. Getting stuck without fuel in some remote area is not what I call fun. If my copilot was to become a bush pilot, I figured this would give him a big boost in experience in how to fly in the North Country.

Caribou season was on, and the seaplane bases were in full swing. The month of August can bring some pretty miserable weather as we experienced a couple of days past, and this day was no exception. We encountered some of the worst weather on our way to Schefferville. Perhaps we should have stayed at the camp.

Blinding snow squalls forced us to fly at tree top level and looking for any lake we could land on. I had to put to test all my experience as a bush pilot. "IFR" flying. I follow the river. I follow the railroad. That's my kind of "IFR" flying. It really stands for Instrument flight rules, but when you're in the North Country anything goes. "Sure!"

One of the major problems flying in the North Country, because there are so many lakes, when the temperature is just right the wind sweeping across the lakes picks up moisture off the water causing continuous snow squalls.

This plays havoc with the bush pilots flying supplies and sportsmen back in the bush. That is why we always stress, bring plenty of extra supplies in case the bush pilot can't get to his destination for a few days.

I personally know of one particular bush pilot that was stranded on a lake high up in the mountains. He made a mistake landing on a high altitude lake that was enclosed with clouds for eleven days. I made three trips up north while all the time he was waiting for the weather to clear. I prefer flying at low altitudes most of the time. I tell everyone I do this because I am afraid of heights.

My friend riding copilot, who wants to be a bush pilot was perhaps wondering if this is what he really wants to be. He would ask " don't you think we had better set this thing down on some lake and wait for the storm to let up?" "If we were back home, no way would you catch me flying in this kind of stuff."

Between using the compass as a rough guide and my luck at being able to map read at such a low level, we finally arrived at the seaplane base in Schefferville. No sooner had we pulled up to the dock and managed to tie down the seaplane we were greeted by several Royal Canadian Mounted Police and game wardens. "We would like to inspect your aircraft and your paper work to see if everything is in order." I swallowed hard, wondering, "what possibly could they find wrong?" With my luck, I can get into trouble without even trying. "Oh well!"

While the three of us stood there speechless I must admit there was a few frantic moments. The Royal Canadian Mounted Police had just seized another aircraft with U.S. registration that was parked at the dock. I overheard someone say the pilot's paperwork wasn't in order so they impounded it. One thing I was careful of, is making sure that I followed the rules as much as possible.

About fifteen minutes had passed before we were given the all clear message. What a relief that was. I have had too many problems with young game wardens trying to make a name for themselves. It was usually an older game warden that came to my rescue and told them to back off. We were told by the Royal Canadian Mounted police that anytime we come into Canada be sure to have our paperwork in order, or else.

Because of all the bad weather and losing some time with the law, our day was slipping by. We needed to refuel the seaplane in a hurry and head for the George River northeast of Schefferville. If things got out hand, we could maybe stay the night at a friend of mine who has an outfitter's camp on Lac Brisson next to the Labrador border. This was mainly for caribou hunting. One end of the lake is in Labrador and the other end in Quebec. Hunters had to be careful not to stray into Labrador with only a Quebec license. One never knows when a game warden will show up, even in the wilds of the North Country.

Due to the height of the caribou season, there was all kinds of commotion going on at the dock on Squaw Lake in Schefferville. It reminded me of the time I drove eighteen hundred miles from New Hampshire to Thunder Bay, Ontario during a blinding blizzard to claim some land the Canadian Government was giving away.

People were using hoods off vehicles to load their gear on and towing them with snowmobiles. Some people tore off through the night for the wilderness half-cocked or drunker than a hoot owl. It was like a bunch of crazy people running all over the place and not knowing what they were doing. They were going to be the first to stake out a piece of land and no one was going to get in their way.

There were certain companies that paid these characters to seek out land in advance and camp on it waiting for the day to come when they can stake out their claim. Helicopters were buzzing here and there when you couldn't see a hand in front you.

This was the way it was at Schefferville. There was every kind of seaplane you could think of coming and going at the dock. What possesses people to act so, I will never know. It's like everyone had a fever of some sort driving them far beyond any point of reasoning. All common sense is left behind when that hunting spirit takes hold.

With the seaplane refueled and ready to go we didn't waste time getting off the lake and heading for Lac Brisson. The weather had cleared to the point of being enjoyable, and was certainly much better flying conditions. The many scattered lakes and rivers passed by under us as we flew over rolling hills and the occasional caribou hunting camps.

It was a sight to see the migrating caribou making their way across the hills, rivers and lakes in a north-westerly direction towards Hudson Bay where they will spend part of the winter, only to return by spring with their newborn.

George River, noted for its Atlantic salmon fishing, loomed up in front of us. It originates approximately one hundred and thirty miles east of Schefferville where hundreds of lakes form the watershed that feeds the George River.

Another huge watershed located a couple of miles east of Schefferville, (Lac Camagoa) forms the River De Pas which joins up with the George River. This all drains to the north into Ungava Bay. It is also a good reason to have a seaplane making it possible to access the vast amount of lakes and rivers in the North

LEARNING TO FLY AND
FISH IN NORTHERN QUEBEC

Country.

For anyone wishing to become a bush pilot, a trip to northern Canada can provide such an unbelievable amount of experience that money just can't buy.

Being able to accompany a full fledged bush pilot that can show how it's done gives you the opportunity to learn in a hurry. Hands on experience is so much better than trying to learn this profession out of a book.

As we fly north up the George River and look into the depths of a few beautiful fishing holes we wish we had purchased a permit for Atlantic salmon fishing. All we could do was to dream about the big fish we could have caught. Perhaps someday, but not on this trip.

It was getting late in the day, so we decided to follow one of the tributaries flowing into the George River over the hills to Lac Brisson. Jack Prudhomme, the owner of a flying service in Quebec called Cargair Ltd., and also the owner of the camp was surprised to see us, but welcomed us to stay for a day or two. It's always helpful to know a few people around the North Country in case you need a favor or two.

Jack had a lot of questions about how many caribou we had seen, and what the weather was down below. We all kind of glanced at each other and smiled as we explained how it was touch and go with the flying into Schefferville. Also, how we were greeted with the Royal Canadian Mounted Police and game wardens. He advised us that they had been patrolling the area around Lac Brisson and along the Labrador border, so be sure to stay away from Labrador. Jack also knew if there were any good fishing holes or hunting areas around the North Country I would find them. Naturally, I would pass on this information to him so he could fly his guests there. In some cases where I had divulged this information to certain seaplane bases thinking I was being a good guy, they would fly people into the area and fish these areas out, ruining the fishing for others. It took me a while to learn my lesson, so since then I have kept my mouth shut.

Staying at the caribou camp that night we got to hear a few stories from the pilots as well as the guests. At times, people stretch their stories so much you wonder whom to believe. Of course all my stories are true, but sound so crazy and far fetched when I tell them to people, they find them hard to believe. Though I lived and experienced such wild adventures for so many years, I question myself if I actually did all these things and lived through it.

The following morning brought us a beautiful day. Who would have thought, that after a few days of blinding snowstorms and big winds, and such horrible flying conditions that the sun would actually shine and be like a summer day.

After a hearty breakfast of bacon and eggs and some home fries it was my job to inspect the seaplane. Before flying out for the day it is always best to check out the floats for water in each compartment, check the gas for any water that could cause frozen gas lines in cold weather, or cause your engine to just plain quit at any moment. Most definitely, the oil should be checked as well as the control surfaces. A pilot would be stupid if he chose to overlook some of these most important items, especially when flying so far from civilization and help.

LEARNING TO FLY AND
FISH IN NORTHERN QUEBEC

It was time to head out for a day of fishing and leave the guys at camp to their caribou hunting. We headed south a few miles to a river flowing out of a large lake. It is one of the tributaries emptying into the George River, but we chose to explore the river near its origination a short distance downstream.

There were many ideal looking fishing holes and rapids, and finding a safe place to land the seaplane was a bit of a problem. We flew up and down the river looking to find a stretch of water big enough to land on without hitting rocks and found an island we could pull up to the shore.

The current in the river was quite strong, which gave me a little problem, but managed to tie up the seaplane safely. One or two casts off of the floats proved to be exciting. We sure hit a beautiful fishing spot. With almost every cast we were hauling in arctic char and trophy size brook trout with an occasional lake trout or salmon.

The river was full of fish. No matter where we cast, a fish would strike our flies. Arctic char with their orange bellies and silvery sides would explode out of the water into the air thrashing about trying to throw the hook to freedom, but one after another fell victim to our fly rods. For those that wanted to swap rods and use a spinning rod, a gold lure with red and black spots worked very well.

Below a waterfall that emptied into a large hole near a ledge produced an unbelievable amount of fishing. We saw hundreds of lake trout, salmon, brook trout, and arctic char in the water hole. Between the four of us, we caught and released at least four hundred fish in one hour. It was like a fish hatchery.

LEARNING TO FLY AND
FISH IN NORTHERN QUEBEC

While we stood there fishing, we watched many caribou walking across the hills. Others made their way to the river's edge to make their way across the river next to us struggling against the strong current. It is so amazing the strength of the caribou and their capability to swim under such adverse conditions. One of the huge bulls came so close to me when he came across the river I thought he was going to run me over. He was probably wondering what kind of an animal I was. He hadn't seen many like me around.

If a person was to ask, "how was the fishing?" I would have to say, "it couldn't get much better." We finished out the day exploring other areas, but did not find the fishing as good as what we had the beginning of the day.

Back at camp that evening, we had some pretty good stories to tell about our fishing excursion. We also enjoyed hearing about some wild stories from the caribou hunters, the shots they missed, and how the caribou managed to disappear so quickly over the horizon. Some of the hunters had bagged a couple of trophy caribou, boasting of their successful hunt.

While everyone was enjoying a home cooked meal we looked out the window to see some caribou walking down the beech next to my seaplane, but no one seem to be too interested in shooting them. Evidently they were too small, and besides they had a few more days to hunt.

This was getting on towards the end of August, which meant cold nights and maybe if your lucky, a few warm days here and there. There remained a few patches of snow along the shore of the lakes and rivers from the winter before. At one point we flew over a herd of caribou gathered on a large patch of snow. Some of the caribou looked ragged and gaunt due to the huge amount of black flies. It seems that the black flies get into the nostrils of the caribou making it hard for the caribou to breathe. It makes them so sick they are unable to eat and therefor starve. I have seen their rib cages sticking out and when they walk they hang their head practically on the ground because they don't have the strength to hold them up.

The caribou seek relief by sticking their nose in the snow which helps drive out the black flies, but this isn't always possible. Then the wolves come and take advantage of the sick and weak caribou that become easy prey.

It's a vicious circle that takes place so much in the North Country. This is one of "Mother Nature's" ways of dealing with things. It helps to control the caribou herd and helps keep the food chain going. What scraps are left over, the black bear will clean up. It seems there is an animal or insect of one kind or the other that will feed on every kind of leftover scraps of a bird, fish, or animal in the world.

After a night's rest, it was decided we would work our way back across the North Country towards my camps. We would explore other fishing areas on the way, hoping to hit a few more hot spots. Fishing for the arctic char was a lot of fun, but seeking out the beautiful speckled brook trout was something I have always enjoyed the most.

The more we flew around the countryside, the more experience my friend gained. I suppose one could say it was a case of on the job training. At times, it was no small feat to land in a section of river, dodging rocks and fighting the strong currents. Learning to judge distance for landing and taking off became an every day ordeal. The more we did the more proficient one becomes.

Flying in the North Country gives a pilot just about every kind of flying condition he or she could ask for. One of the biggest challenges is landing and taking off on a river surrounded by high mountains. Wind gusts present such a problem, at times it can be very dangerous. When coming in for a landing down between the mountains, the wind gusts can flip the seaplane in a split second. Other times, it can present an updraft lifting the seaplane forty-five hundred feet so quick, all you can do is to hang on and ride it out.

I remember a time when some friends and I were caribou hunting and camping out on the Caniapiscau River, a wicked snowstorm hit us with all its fury. Talk about the wrath of "Mother Nature," well we sure got it this time. For three days we couldn't make it back to camp. Big winds and snow so thick we couldn't see a hand in front of us kept us from flying. The wind blew so strong we had to anchor the tent down with rocks and logs for fear it would blow into the river. Thank god for warm sleeping bags.

One of my friends kept saying "were going to die, we will never make it out of here alive." Food was running so short it got so one of the fellows was stealing my food out of my bag and hiding it in his. Panic had set in, but this guy was from the city and had no idea how to survive when the going got tough. I tried my best to settle him down, but he was hard to convince he would live to see another day and get back to his family safe and sound.

LEARNING TO FLY AND
FISH IN NORTHERN QUEBEC

We had killed a caribou, so it wasn't a case where we were going to starve. It was tough getting a fire going with all the wet conditions, but placing some rocks around an open fire got them hot enough to cook on and have some delicious steaks. I never flew anywhere without taking some salt and pepper with me for a little seasoning. One never knows when you may have to use it.

When we got a little break in the weather I figured I would try and get us back to camp, but every time we would take off we would fly into another snowstorm. No matter what I did, or how hard I would try, I could not penetrate the snowstorm enough to get through to the camp. I was forced to turn back to where we had been camped.

As I dropped down over the mountains into the valley below to land on the river, strong wind gusts blew us about like a cork in an ocean storm. First, there would be an updraft, then a downdraft would throw the seaplane all about. All my expertise as a bush pilot was being put to the test. Years of flying was telling me not to overshoot the landing spot on the river, or we would slam into the mountainside

The river was very narrow where I had to land. I had to come over the river at an angle and kick the tail of the seaplane around at the last minute and dump the plane onto the water to get stopped in a hurry before hitting the rocks on the shore.

Just as I was about to touch down a huge gust lifted the seaplane up and slammed it down in a matter of seconds. I killed the power and hoped for the best bringing the seaplane to a halt within inches from the rocks on the shore. You can be sure, whenever you fly around a mountain area caution must be used because most always there will be wind conditions to deal with. Some can be fatal.

In time, the snowstorm subsided and we were able to make it back to camp. Just for kicks, I thought I would throw this little episode in.

Due to the geographical layout of certain areas, it makes a big difference in the kind of fish one may catch, or the type of fishing. Some areas surrounded by bogs and shallow water will not produce the kind of speckled brook trout fishing I am used to.

As I have mentioned before, when I fly around the North Country searching for that likely fishing spot, I look for the large lakes with connecting rivers that have beautiful sets of rapids and deep holes that will more than likely provide some excellent fishing.

Learning to map read is a very important part of flying, especially in the north far from civilization. If you don't know where you are, or can't find your way around, you could be in serious trouble. You could get lost and run out of fuel trying to find your way back into civilization. But in the case where a pilot sets out to do a little exploring for trout fishing, it's nice to know how to map read to get to some of those secret holes.

We headed for a river that flows into Hudson Bay. As we passed over vast uninhabited land scattered with thousands of lakes and rivers, the mountains gave way to many rolling hills and low land.

I had my sights set on a particular area where there was a large river. It flowed from one large lake to another. Flying low over the river gave us a bird's eye view enabling us to pick out the many rapids and waterholes.

LEARNING TO FLY AND
FISH IN NORTHERN QUEBEC

By now, my friend wanting to become a bush pilot was building more and more experience. He was so amazed at the ease I could set the seaplane down in about any place I wanted to. Learning to memorize where the rocks are in the river along with the wind directions and the effects of the hills surrounding your landing area plays a big part in a bush pilots profession.

It is not always possible to totally read the wind conditions, but at least flying around the area you are to land in and reading the surface of the water can alert a pilot in a general sense.

What I am about to tell you, is perhaps in every fisherman's dream. Speckled brook trout lurked in the waters below like you would never believe. As we approached the landing spot looking down into the beautiful pristine waters, speckled brook trout went scurrying to different corners of the river. We couldn't wait to wet out lines.

Rushing to tie the seaplane safely to the bank of the river brought anxious moments. "Hurry up, everyone was saying, let's go get em." "I can't wait to catch one of them babies." As each fly gently rested on the surface of the river, a monstrous brook trout rose to take the fly. In an instant, all heck broke loose. Trout were running from one part of the river to another. "Get the net, here's another." "What are you waiting for?" It was clear that their was plenty of excitement.

Looking down into the depths of the river and seeing such a beautiful sight with all those red bellied trout swimming around, brought to mind my conversations with other sportsmen of how they wished they could experience this kind of fishing.

LEARNING TO FLY AND
FISH IN NORTHERN QUEBEC

We thought we had good fishing over next to the Labrador border, but this was something else. Catching brook trout up to eleven pounds or so wasn't too hard to take. Nobody was complaining about the fishing. If ever a person wanted to get away to do a little fishing where you don't have to compete for a fishing spot, this was it.

How many times did we watch a huge trout swim by and take a quick glance up at our fly without making a spiral up to the surface of the water. Some of the people I tell my stories to, ask, "how come we didn't meet you years ago?" "If we had only known."

As life goes on, and time slips by, I often wonder, "will I ever get a chance to do some more of what I have enjoyed so much?" The older we get, the harder it becomes to pass your flight physical, shortening the days that you can fly. So I guess it nice to take advantage of an offer to fly up north and do some fishing when you can.

It's time to say goodbye to a wonderful day of fishing and head back to camp. The week was coming to a close and we have a long flight back. Here's hoping the good weather lasts. I am sure this is one trip my friend that wants to become a bush pilot will remember for a long time.

FIRE
IN THE NORTH

It seemed that old "Mother Nature" was busy doing her thing again. I was heading out for another fishing excursion, but decided it was best to check out the weather situation up north. With all the sudden weather changes going on, there was no need to take extra chances.

Flying from New Hampshire to our chosen destination seven and one half-hours flying time to northern Quebec had brought many challenges in the past, but what I was about to hear was something entirely different.

Thunderstorms had set off hundreds of forest fires all over northern Quebec. From the information I got in the report about the fires, I figured I had better pick a different flight path. Just maybe, if we were lucky, we could skirt some of the worst of the fires and make it through to my camps by the Caniapiscau River.

I explained the situation to my friends, but that didn't seem to sway their minds much. They wanted to go fishing and they probably thought if I was willing to go I must know what I was doing. When someone has scheduled a particular time off, it's hard to change it.

It was still early in the morning and with the 206 Cessna on floats parked at my brother's dock on Lake Sunapee we proceeded to pack our gear aboard the seaplane. Heavy items were packed toward the front as close to the passenger seats as possible, and the lighter gear towards the rear. This was necessary for the weight and balance of the aircraft.

FIRE
IN THE NORTH

With full fuel tanks and extra gas in seven-gallon plastic containers on board, we lifted off Lake Sunapee headed for Quebec City via Lake Memphremagog, just over the Canadian line from Newport, Vermont. The plan was to fly to Quebec City, cut across the Laurentide Mountains and up to Lake St. Jean.

Not realizing how serious the forest fires were, we found ourselves flying through smoke so thick we were forced to fly at tree top level in order to see where we were going. Map reading became almost impossible because of the visibility. As it is, the Laurentide Mountains are treacherous to fly through in normal bad weather because of their high mountains and valleys and wind conditions.

I figured it was best to keep going, rather than land in some lake and get stuck there with all the fires and smoke. Talk about tough flying conditions, I think I would rather fly through snowstorms than forest fires.

I found myself relying on my compass more than ever before. At least it gave me a rough guide as far as keeping on course as much as possible. Time crept by slowly as we punched our way towards the north through the thick smoke and haze, wondering if we were ever going to get into the clear. What was in reality, two to three hours of flying seemed more like an eternity.

When we finally did break out into the clear, we found ourselves over Lake St. Jean. I knew of a small seaplane base at the north end of the lake and suggested we had better land there and top off the fuel tanks in case we got into trouble further north. It would be a mistake to run out of fuel dodging forest fires and wonder if you are ever going to get rescued.

FIRE
IN THE NORTH

We landed at the seaplane base to refuel only to find it deserted. Either the owner and pilots were on vacation, or they had all gone north fishing. I thought it strange that nobody was around to sell fuel. I walked around looking for someone, but resorted to walking to a house down the road to inquire as to where everyone was.

After two or three phone calls we finally managed to locate a person to do with the seaplane base. We had lost valuable time, as we didn't know for sure what the conditions were further north as far as the forest fires were concerned. Because of the distance we had to fly to my camp we needed to get away in a hurry.

The lake at the seaplane base was fairly small, and with the big load in the seaplane, I was wondering, if in fact, we could get up enough speed to clear the trees at the other end of the lake. There was no measured runway strip here, and one mistake could end our fishing trip in a hurry.

I knew my 206 Cessna pretty well and it responded to my demands equally. Taxiing to the furthest most point at the south end of the lake gave us just enough edge to make it safely off the lake. My friends sweat a little as we narrowly missed the treetops, but that's the name of the game when you are a bush pilot. If only we didn't need to fly so far north to go fishing we would not have to carry all the extra gear.

We had been warned to steer clear of any area where forest fires were, but they were all over the place, how could we avoid them if we wanted to go north. So we flew on our merry way. The further north we flew, I knew there were many more lakes. Some

The Adventures of a Bush Pilot II

Wow!! Richard told me they come big in Northern Quebec... a lake trout weighing 43 lbs.

An old warrior brook trout weighing 9 pounds and 6 ounces.

The Adventures of a Bush Pilot II

Paradise! In the area of Hudson Bay. One of author's secret fishing holes.

The results of but another successful caribou hunting trip.

The Adventures of a Bush Pilot II

Women also enjoy fishing. Author's wife in Northern Quebec with her catch.

Having fun in Northern Quebec.

The Adventures of a Bush Pilot II

Doing it the hard way! Author carrying the head and cape of 1600 pound moose.

Picture painted by author of caribou migrating.

FIRE
IN THE NORTH

large and some small, but much more than in the southern area. This meant if worse came to worse we could find safety among the lakes in the north.

That's not exactly how it turned out. All those lakes didn't amount to "hoorah" as far as the fires goes. The wind was causing the fire to jump from one lake to the other, burning everything in its path. Sporting camps went up in flames in a matter of minutes stranding several sportsmen and all we could see was charred territory.

I guess we should have stayed home, but most of the time the Canadian Government prefers to let these fires burn out on their own unless they are threatening civilization. Perhaps that is why there are so many blueberries in the north. Usually where there has been a forest fire, a lot of blueberry bushes spring up.

Fighting our way through smoke and haze was no small fete. Between the poor visibility and breathing all that smoke, we had all we wanted to deal with. It was uncomforting to think my camps would be burned, but they were on an island in the middle of a large lake and I could only pray they would be okay.

Fires continued to rage throughout our flight north. We were only a few miles from my camps when much to my surprise the forest fire had burned only to one small mountain just short of the camps. What a sigh of relief that was. We could finally breathe fresh air for a change and actually see the horizon to the north.

By this time, it was getting late in the day, and arriving at camp before darkness overtook us was a godsend. A good hot supper and a relaxing evening brought a lot of conversation about where we were going to fish the following day. We were weary from the long flight, and a long night's sleep would sure feel good. Flying through all that forest fire business gave me quite a workout, so what we had in store for the next day would bring quite a change.

The following morning brought us a beautiful sun shiny day. The smoke filled skies of the day before had given way to the north winds clearing the air and giving us visibility beyond the horizon. Most of the territory north of the camp was barren and gave little chance for forest fires so we felt comfortable flying a few hundred miles north of the camp. We would explore more fishing areas.

With a good breakfast of home fries and bacon and eggs under our belt, we loaded up the seaplane and headed for the wide open spaces of the north. The beautiful moss covered rolling hills and scattered lakes was a sight to see. Every river we passed over had us asking the question, "I wonder how the fishing is down there?" "I'll bet there's some big old speckled trout in one those holes. Maybe we could stop on the way back if we have time."

We came upon an old abandoned camp that looked like it had been deserted for years. Red squirrels had made a home there and whatever food supplies were left they had gotten into. Dishes were still on the table with scraps of food scattered about and coffee cups half full. There wasn't much left for us to munch on, but I don't know as I would have eaten it anyway.

Whoever was planning on coming back to this camp never made it. There was two-way radio equipment on a table in the corner of the camp and outside in the bushes was stashed a couple of snowmobiles.

FIRE
IN THE NORTH

While poking around the area outside the camp, I came upon an old canoe tied bottom-side up between two trees and a rusty looking rifle tie underneath. It appeared, that either the Indian, Eskimo, or person to do with this camp must have died, or he forgot where his camp was. It also is possible that the person or people may have died in a plane crash bringing to an end any knowledge of the whereabouts of the camp.

This sort of thing happens in the north and occasionally someone like myself stumbles onto one of these camps and takes them over. Thus, the challenge of the north continues, especially for those that like to explore new territory.

It's quite interesting trying to figure out what happened to people in such cases. After close scrutinizing and a little investigating you can piece together the picture of perhaps what happened. It's the same thing when we stumble onto an aircraft that crashed on a sandbar or in the rapids of a river. We look around for human skeletons or some sign of survival.

Sometimes when I check out the engine of a crashed airplane and see a broken connecting rod sticking through the block, it's not too hard to figure why the airplane crashed. Then you look over the situation further to see how damaged the cockpit is to determine if a person actually got killed or was able to walk away. Some of these people that try to walk out are never heard from since. They just disappear in the north to whatever their fate.

As interesting as it may be locating some of these abandoned camps, our main goal is to keep looking for that illusive brook trout, the wold record. Out there somewhere, there is a fishing hole I haven't discovered yet. I know if I keep looking, I will find it unless I get too old to travel. But after all, what are dreams for. It is something to look forward to, to occupy my mind during the long cold winter months.

Flying into the many different rivers in the North Country gave me a big thrill. The challenge of landing in the swift currents, or rocky rivers kept me sharp. I knew what I could do with my seaplane, and with some luck, I could push things to the edge and get away with it without endangering my passengers.

I never felt I could depend on someone else to get me out of trouble, so whatever challenge I decided to take on, I was the one that had to deal with it. Once I made a decision, I had to see it through, and hoped it to be the right one.

The one big thing I had going for me, was the fact that the 206 Cessna and me were a team, and a good one. Times when the old adrenaline was working there wasn't much stopping me from going into places like beaver dams and real small ponds. I know of other bush pilots with DeHavilland Beavers that just plain refused to go into some of the places that I had.

Did I mention that the man upstairs had made a deal with me. That he would ride on my shoulders and watch over me all the years that I flew so I could get away with some of my flying antics. Maybe that's how I am able to get more terrific trout fishing because no one else dares to go into the places that I go .

One of these places happened to be by the River LaGrande that flowed west into Hudson Bay. The river was rampant with the high water due to a lot of rain and at the base of a waterfall there was a large hole. As we flew over the area I studied the river closely looking for rocks and a strip of water long enough to land on without wrecking the seaplane. Slowly I set the seaplane down in the swift waters taking care not to get caught up in the current and get swept over the waterfalls. No matter how good a pilot may be, there is always that one time the law of average catches up with him.

One of the important parts of seaplane flying is to be able to safely taxi the seaplane to the shore or dock and secure it. Luck was on our side this time. We got out the fishing rods and proceeded down the edge of the waterfall. The water spray was shooting high in the air and wetting the rocks on the side of the river making them very slippery.

One slip and it could spell catastrophe. With the raging waters and being so cold, it would be very difficult to survive very long. I suggested we do the buddy system where two people stay near each other in case the other gets into trouble. The rough waters made it almost impossible to tell when we had a fish on the line.

After spending a while fishing, it was decided we would get out of this place before we pushed our luck a little too much and check out another river. This time, we hit the jackpot. There were brook trout just about every where we cast. Three to five pound brook trout were common to catch, but when we hooked into trout up to eight and nine pounds things livened up.

I had seen plenty of what I call excellent trout fishing in the past and I would have to say this would place pretty high in a fisherman's expectations. Once in a while we would hook into a nice salmon or lake trout, but when we saw the deep red bellies of a

FIRE
IN THE NORTH

speckled brook trout rise to the surface and make a roll after taking a fly, that was what we came north for.

We had spent the day flying around checking out different rivers and their rapids but it was time to head south back to camp. I had used up a good amount of fuel and hoped we would have enough for the trip back. A bush pilot never knows what he may encounter flying around the north so he has to be ready for just about anything. Therefore, he should allow extra time for a flight of any distance.

When the weather is nice it is absolutely a pleasure to fly around the North Country. It is such a contrast compared to fighting snowstorms or flying through rain and fog at tree top level.

There were times when I would land the seaplane on some beautiful remote lake surrounded by rolling hills. We would break out some vitals and kick back in amazement, to think, "here we are way up in gods country away from the hectic life of the cities and nobody to bother us." It is a kind of life I will always remember. I couldn't forget it very well, for almost on a nightly basis I live it in my dreams. Perhaps one day I will get a phone call that will tell me to go down to the dock, there is a Cessna 206 on floats waiting for me. It's mine, enjoy.

Well, as you may guess, the wind had changed from the south and as we arrived at camp the sky was filled with smoke from the still lingering forest fires to the south. We had our fun up north and decided to head home the first thing in the morning. Only this time we would take a different route. After all we had been through and done, the guys were ready to head home.

FIRE
IN THE NORTH

In the north, you are lucky if you get a couple of good days in a row. When I looked out the window of the camp to the east early in the morning, the sky was just as beautiful and pink as all get out. No need to tell you what that means, but I knew we were in trouble weather wise. Usually, within one hour of flying time heading south of the camps, we will run smack dab into a miserable storm and that is exactly what happened.

Playing Russian Roulette with fog patches and heavy rain is not exactly fun. By flying south along the sixty-ninth longitude we could get around most of the forest fires. They would be mostly to the west of our fight path. Not only that, but we would be flying over a series of lakes and rivers giving us a place to land in case I couldn't make it through some of the stormy conditions.

A friend of mine decided he wanted to follow me home, but let me tell you, when I am flying in bad weather, I don't like trying to keep track of another airplane. It is distracting as all get out, and I have my hands full as it is.

Because of the bad foggy conditions, we were forced to land on a lake high in the hills. Both seaplanes were loaded to the hilt, which meant someone was going to have a hard time taking off when the conditions improved.

It was several hours later before we decided to try and head south for Bae Comeau. We had taxied to the north end of the lake so to get all the room possible for takeoff. One of the main problems for taking off was, the lake was calm as can be. The glassy water is very difficult to take off on. There is no wind to give the seaplane that added lift. With a big load it compounds the problem and sometimes I have had to unload several items in order to lessen the weight and get off the water.

By staying in radio contact with my pilot friend, I figured we could keep in touch and know what the other is doing and where he is. I had managed to get off the lake and circled around watching for my friend to take off, but all the while I circled over the lake it seemed my friend was having a tough time of it. I knew if I continued flying around too much, I would use up too much fuel and not have enough to get to Bae Comeau. I didn't want to land back at the lake so all I could do was to hope my friend could make it off at one point or the other and head south.

It was tough battling the fog and rain where the visibility was down to nil. Minutes later, we were flying between the banks of the river just over the water when we finally approached the Manicougan Reservoir. This is a huge body of water with a large island in the middle. To give you an idea of how big it is, it takes about two hours to fly around it. Years ago a large meteor created it.

If the weather was ever going to be bad, it was in the area of the Manicouagan Reservoir. We had dropped from a few hundred feet down to the very level of the reservoir. When the visibility got so bad I couldn't see the propeller I figured it was time to land the seaplane.

Rather than to just sit there and wait it out, I chose to taxi in a southerly direction through the fog. I couldn't see the shoreline and had to watch out for trees that stuck up out of the water.

FIRE
IN THE NORTH

Ledges that poked up out of the water was another concern. I had to watch that we didn't run into one of them for fear of damaging a float. With one person standing on the float guiding me and watching for trees and ledges, it seemed like two hours had passed before the fog dissipated somewhat.

It was now getting late in the day. We had lost a lot of time fooling around in the bad weather. The fog had lifted just enough to allow me to takeoff, but had to keep low over the water. I couldn't get altitude enough to clear the trees and the ledges sticking out of the water so had to go around them.

For a while it was tricky flying, but that was nothing compared to later on. When we got to the mouth of the river where it flows out of the reservoir, we were back into thick fog. The floats were just about touching the surface of the water as we approached the Manic Five Dam.

With the fog half way down my windshield and the floats practically dragging on the water I swung wide close to the shore of the river just at the top of the dam so I could get a good look at the next level of the river below the dam.

It was about five hundred feet down over the dam and the trick was to be able to see the river under the fog. I didn't think I wanted to dive the seaplane over the face of the dam unless I could see underneath the fog. Good thinking Richard.

I hadn't heard a word from my friend with the other seaplane. I kept trying to reach him on the radio, but no response. At this point, he was on his own. Flying between the riverbanks kept me on my toes. I hoped

FIRE
IN THE NORTH

the fellows with me were getting a big kick out it. After what seemed an eternity, we finally arrived at the seaplane base at Bae Comeau. There were seaplanes parked all over the place. It appeared that the weather had been really bad down south of where we were and fourteen seaplanes had been stuck there for four days. When we did manage to find a spot to tie the seaplane up, a group of pilots came rushing over asking, "how's the weather up north?" I remarked, "real ducky." Of course, I was kidding. They were all waiting for the weather to clear so they could head home towards Montreal.

Being close to dark, we hitched a ride into the town of Bae Comeau to stay the night. To my surprise, my friend with the other seaplane shows up. He managed to finally get off the lake up on the mountain and make it to a small seaplane base to the west of Manic Five Dam. He had to refuel in order to make it to Bae Comeau. The weather had cleared enough to let him down through. Bush flying sure has its challenges.

Come morning we thought we would get an early start for home, but the storm still persisted. Fog banks along the St. Lawrence River were bound to give us a problem. The fourteen pilots decided they wanted to follow me back to Montreal. I told myself I must be crazy to agree to keep in radio contact with all of these guys. Some couldn't speak any English, and I could only speak a little French. This was going to be something else.

Can you imagine fifteen airplanes flying around in the fog following the St. Lawrence River and a bunch of jibber-jabbering going on over the radio. And I thought keeping track of one or two airplanes was too much.

FIRE
IN THE NORTH

Somebody was going to get lost, and that is what happened. Over the radio comes the message. "I'm lost, I don't know where I am.

Four airplanes got lost that day and to this day, I don't know if they made it to Montreal, or not. It's a wonder anybody made it through. I had to land in the middle of the St. Lawrence River where the fog was so thick I couldn't see to taxi to shore. The best thing I could do was to taxi by instrument tuned in to an airport up river until I got out of the fog. I don't know if the black whales thought I was one of them or not, but it seemed we were playing touch and go for a while. In the process, we managed to get stuck on a sand-bar, but were able to get out and shove the seaplane back into deep water.

Needless to say, with all the wild life around the St. Lawrence River and the challenge of flying through so much bad weather made the trip home quite interesting. We had managed to keep clear of the forest fires that had been dampened by a few days rain and make it safely back to New Hampshire. I always say, "if you ever want a few thrills and a little excitement in your life, become a bush pilot."

THE RIGORS
OF CARIBOU HUNTING

Each year during the months of August and September it becomes many a sportsman's dream to partake in a caribou hunt. The rigors involved in one of these hunts, if only known to many of these sportsmen involved while in the chase, would certainly have second thoughts about leaving home.

Caribou hunting in northern Quebec can be a lot of fun and very exciting. On the other hand, it can bring catastrophe like no one ever dreamed. From many years of experience in the North Country, I can tell you it is one heck of an experience if things don't work out like you planned.

Some friends of mine wanted me to take them caribou hunting. I said, "sure, meet at Lake Sunapee and I will give you a trip of a lifetime." I had just gotten off one trip where we had run into some bad weather. This time, it was a mixture of rain and snow. We had flown north of the Caniapiscau River in some of the most miserable weather I had ever seen.

Rain, snow, and big winds made it so tough flying, I was looking for the first safe lake to land on. It was late September, so it wasn't exactly a surprise to see so much bad weather. Though I have seen a warming trend up north since back in the sixties, northern Quebec can still have its surprises.

THE RIGORS
OF CARIBOU HUNTING

We had been flying through fog, rain, and snow to get to the area where we wanted to caribou hunt. Trying to fly and map read at the same time through and around so much bad weather was a big challenge in itself. I was forced to fly through valleys and around the hills at ground level, and at the same time, try to keep water under us in case we had to land the seaplane in a hurry.

It was decided we would land on a large lake surrounded by mountains. The only safe place to park the seaplane was a small beach on the east shore of the lake. Most of the shoreline around the lake was too rocky to take a chance on damaging the floats.

The only dry spot available to set up the tent was on the small beach. Everywhere on the side of the mountain the ground was saturated from the heavy rain, which made it virtually impossible to set up the tent on high ground. Streams of water came tumbling down from the mountainside. It's a good thing we had our hip boots with us.

We had only time enough before dark to cook up a meal, but getting a fire going in all the wet conditions was tough. I had to drain some fuel out of my wing tank to get the fire going, and even then it was a struggle to keep it going.

I knew the beach was pretty much at water level, but who would ever have dreamt that the wind would change directions during the night. Talk about being uncomfortable, that beach didn't have a soft spot on it. Not only that, but somehow, the rain found its way into the tent and everything got soaked. What a way to start out on a caribou hunt. The wind howled and blew so much during the night, I thought for a minute

THE RIGORS
OF CARIBOU HUNTING

or two the tent was going to be blown upon the mountaintop. No one got much sleep trying to find a dry spot in the tent.

Evidently, the wind had changed directions during the night bringing high winds out of the west sweeping huge waves across the lake lashing out at the tent and totally swamping it. We managed to scrounge up some rocks to help hold the tent down.

Come morning, there was a few cold, wet bodies standing around a campfire. The rigors of a caribou hunting trip had already taken its toll. How anyone can say they could enjoy a trip to this degree, I'll never know. This was a far cry from the comforts of home, back in civilization.

Being grounded because of such severe storms sort of takes the fun out of hunting. After getting our clothes dried, we grabbed our rifles and made our way up the mountain. Very few caribou were seen due to the sudden change in weather, which led us to believe we had better not be too fussy. The meat tastes just as good, whether it was from a big trophy bull, or a female. In fact, the Indians prefer eating the female caribou.

It seems to be one of "Mother Nature's" ways of clearing the air of storms with a strong northwesterly wind. It can push the storms out in a hurry, so if you see the wind change from the south to out of the northwest you can expect good weather in a short time.

We stood on the mountain watching the weather clear before our eyes. The caribou had taken shelter from the wind, lying on the leeward side of the hills and in some of the low areas. When we poked our

THE RIGORS
OF CARIBOU HUNTING

heads over the mountain, several caribou jumped to their feet and took off like a streak of lightning down over the open mountainside.

The next few moments was filled with the sharp sound of rifles firing away. The bullets had found their mark on two of the big bulls in the group as they went crashing to the ground. Other caribou scattered in all directions and went charging down off the mountain. Some headed down along the lakeshore, while part of the group headed across the lake swimming against the big wind and waves.

Shooting a caribou or moose is one thing, but the big job is to dress the animal and quarter it, then get it out to where you can load it into the seaplane. It takes a strong back and perseverance to lug these animals a great distance. Sometimes, I think it's a case of all brawn and no brain. Just imagine how many people pay big bucks to go out there and break their back running up and down the mountains and hauling out their game.

Our hunt was over, and getting all the gear packed away and the caribou reloaded with a tarpaulin wrapped around them before another storm snuck in on us was a priority. I don't like taking chances with meat spoiling, so whenever the weather is good enough to head home I try to take advantage of it. I was coming back up north for one last caribou trip as soon as I got back off of this one.

To make this story short, I had gotten my friends and their caribou home safely, only to have two more friends waiting on my doorstep to make a return trip. It was like a summer day at home, gentle breezes and warm weather, just the kind of day I enjoy flying. What

THE RIGORS
OF CARIBOU HUNTING

I wouldn't give to have one more week like this. The guys were anxious to get going, but I needed a little rest and had to have a day to check out the seaplane to make sure everything was okay with it. There was no sense of taking extra chances when a little preventative maintenance might keep you out of trouble.

I needed to get a fresh change of clothes and shop for some groceries. The seaplane needed refueling, the oil had to be changed, plus a good general checkover. Making sure the seaplane is in good shape was a priority in my life, and it might just mean my life some day, if you know what I mean.

If I got stuck in sub freezing weather up north, a fresh change of oil could make a big difference in hand propping the engine in case of a dead battery.

The following morning I was greeted at my brother's dock on Lake Sunapee where I keep my seaplane by my two anxious friends. I had to sort out their baggage and leave behind what I call excess baggage. That's one good way to lose a few friends, telling them you don't need this or that. I usually have to tell them, "you have to make up your mind if you want to take all this extra stuff, or leave room to bring a few caribou back." That usually convinces them.

No matter what the weather was up north the week before, it still was a relief to be heading back into god's country. I hoped that the good weather would last for a few days, but I guess I was mistaken. We had managed to get to Bae Comeau okay, but as we approached my camps up by the Caniapiscau River, things took a drastic turn for the worse. It was like jumping from summer into the middle of the winter.

THE RIGORS
OF CARIBOU HUNTING

In just the two days since I left the North Country it had snowed about four feet. All of the outfitters had closed their camps and flown the coup. A blizzard had hit the North Country with such fury, it drove everyone out, if they could get out.

Most of the smaller lakes were frozen over and only a few of the larger lakes were still open. Being so late in the day, it was foolish to fly any further north, so it was best that we stay at camp that night. Getting an early start in the morning would give us plenty of daylight to do our thing. Plus the fact, we had no idea what the weather conditions were going to be north of the camp.

After a cold, blustery night, we were lucky to get the seaplane cranked up and deiced. Between having to hack the ice off the floats and getting all the snow off the wings it was a nasty preparation to depart for the north. We lost valuable time, but we were thankful to be on our way. From all the signs, I knew we were going to be in for one rough trip.

We had another two to three hundred miles to go to get up into caribou country and lord only knows what we were going to run into for weather. The first hundred miles took us over small rolling hills, but after that, we had to fly over some rugged mountains, taking us up into the thick of a snowstorm.

Having to dodge the mountains while flying through the snow was no picnic. I had to keep my wits about me at all times and hoped we got into better going.

As we flew further north toward the De Lay River, all we could see was barren land covered with snow. Not an animal was stirring in the vast wilderness of the north. There were snowdrifts up to eight feet deep

THE RIGORS
OF CARIBOU HUNTING

on the sides of the mountains where the wind had blown so hard, that it blew most of the snow off the mountain tops.

The thought came over my mind, "what in the world am I doing back up in this god for saken country in this kind of weather?" I should have known better than to come back up here so late in the season, but here we are.

There were no caribou to be seen anywhere. It was like the whole herd of caribou had long since migrated through the area. It was like a ghost town completely deserted. There were no wolf tracks or bear tracks. Usually, the wolves tend to follow the migration of the caribou as I have seen many times in the past. Where could they all have gone in such a few days? Due to the severe weather change, the bear must have gone into hibernation.

I remembered the location of an outfitter's camp not far from where we were, and decided we should go there. At least we would have some shelter while we poked around looking for caribou. The next thing was to fight our way through the storm and find the camp.

If a person was to ask me what kind of a challenge do I find my life as a bush pilot, I would have to say, "it certainly has its moments." But after all, what fun would there be without fighting the elements that old "Mother Nature" throws at me once in a while. That's what keeps me going.

We eventually found our way through the mountains and valleys and over lakes and rivers to the camp. The camp was damp and cold like an iceberg, showing signs of desertion. An hour or two later, we had a rip roaring fire going in the old cast iron stove

THE RIGORS
OF CARIBOU HUNTING

supported by four stubby legs sitting on a piece of metal for safety. Along both inside walls of the camp there were two rows of double bunks capable of sleeping about sixteen people. A gas lamp provided the lighting. Under a section of the floor was a box for storing a few supplies.

There has to be an outhouse of some sort and that was located up the hill a little ways from the camp. This was to be a big surprise come morning. It had been a long weary day and the guys were tuckered out from all the day's excitement. I guess no matter if a person is flying the airplane, or just a passenger, the stress of dealing with all the bad weather had taken its toll.

After downing some pork and beans and having a few discussions, everyone hit the sack. We wondered what the next day would bring as everyone wasn't in the best of moods. Nobody had much hopes of getting a caribou after seeing no sign of any life around. It's a known fact that when I go after a certain kind of game or fish, I most generally have success.

Come morning, I found out that an outhouse is good for more than one thing. At the crack of dawn I decided I would crawl out of the sack and have a look around, but the first thing in order was to hit the outhouse for a little relief.

The inside of the camp sounded like a small logging operation with all the snoring going on and I didn't figure I should wake anyone for what I had to do. I grabbed my rifle and quietly snuck out the door of the camp to make my way to the outhouse. Tall brush overhung both sides of the narrow trail going to the outhouse obstructing my view of the surrounding

THE RIGORS
OF CARIBOU HUNTING

area. The heavy frost on the branches sparkled in the morning sun and the snow covered ground seemed so pure and pristine. With a roll of toilet paper in one hand and my trusty 308 Savage in the other, I strolled nonchalantly up the trail. What took place in the next few moments nobody would believe in a million years.

Towering above those frosty branches were several huge trophy antlers belonging to some big old bull caribou. I couldn't believe my eyes. I forgot all about visiting the outhouse and made an about-face quietly making my way back to the camp.

I barged through the door waking up the gang as I walked next to their bunks dragging them out of their sleeping bags. I yelled in a low tone, "caribou, caribou, get your guns, they're just outside the camp, hurry."

One of the guys didn't even bother putting on his pants, he went out the doorway in his long johns. The other made his way along the lakeshore. In a matter of minutes it was all over. Everyone filled their tags and was so surprised how it all happened, they would talk about this one for quite some time.

The job of quartering the caribou was done in a hurry and in order to help keep the meat from spoiling on the way home we put the meat in the icy water of the lake. That chills the meat in a short time getting all the body heat out of the meat. Packing the meat between a tarpaulin helps keep it clean as well as helping to keep our gear from getting soiled.

I have never seen anyone wanting to get out of the North Country in such a hurry as these fellows. They didn't want to stick around for another blizzard. If all went well, we could make our way south into warmer

THE RIGORS
OF CARIBOU HUNTING

territory where the lakes wouldn't be frozen over. I know these kind of stories might tend to discourage a few people from wanting to go caribou hunting, but some people would refuse to believe these sort of things can happen in the north.

Flying for so many years as I have as a bush pilot and guide has brought many a story. Some are believable, and some not so believable. I guess that's why my body is so full of aches and pains, because I have pushed it to the extreme.

After having such wild episodes of flying in the North Country it is always nice to get my passengers, or sports as you may call them, back home safely to their loved ones. So they may tell their grandchildren of their great caribou hunting trip and that wild bush pilot they flew with. At least I am still alive to tell about it, where so many other bush pilots didn't survive.

Occasionally, I meet some of the people I have flown throughout the years. They remind me of the fantastic trip they had and the trophy fish or game they bagged. When I sit back and relive some of my adventures, I kind of chuckle to myself and say, "gee, did I really do all those things." It is something to think about in my next life.

BUSH PILOTING
IN NEW ENGLAND

For the pilots wishing to become a bush pilot, New England could be their place to get started. New Hampshire and Maine are fortunate to have many bodies of water where a pilot with a seaplane can enjoy his or hers life.

I was never lucky to have a lake next to my back yard so I could look out my window and see my 206 Cessna parked at the dock. The next best thing was to have a brother that owned some lake frontage and a dock big enough to keep my seaplane at. I give thanks to my brother for allowing me to do that.

New England has the geographical layout to make bush flying an interesting profession or hobby. With all the wildlife, such as moose, deer and bear, it gives pilots and their friends something extra to do. Over the years, spotting and photographing moose has been a great past time in New Hampshire and Maine.

Flying around the White Mountains and Mt. Washington can be a challenge for the average pilot due to gusty winds and strong updrafts and downdrafts. Caution should always be exercised when flying in mountainous areas. As a rule, the higher one flies the stronger the winds. Seaplanes can also provide a margin of safety being able to land on just about any body of water, unless it happens to be a small beaver dam tucked away on the side of a mountain.

BUSH PILOTING
IN NEW ENGLAND

Though I have landed on some of them up in Canada, I don't advise it for the average pilot. New England is a beautiful area with its many rivers stretching from north to south.

The Connecticut River flows all the way from near the Quebec border in northern New Hampshire to the ocean in Connecticut. It is amazing how many seaplanes one finds parked on a small pond or lake throughout New England. It may be a Piper Cub, or it could be a Cessna 206.

Many pilots find that a 172 Cessna is economical and easy to fly, but if they want a little more horsepower a 180 or 185 Cessna will do the job.

Pilots flying a seaplane with straight floats find it more difficult to get fuel. The availability of fuel is far less because of fewer seaplane bases versus airports. Airplanes with amphibious floats (wheels built into the floats) are more versatile, but the problem with them is, it cuts down the capacity to carry a bigger load.

Getting to know where to refuel a seaplane is quite often a bit of a hassle. A lot of times seaplane bases marked on a flight map no longer exist. Like when I flew to Alaska, three quarters of the seaplane bases marked on the new maps I had just purchased had been out of existence for several years.

When flying such a distance across a vast wilderness a pilot needs to know where he can refuel. Getting stuck in some remote area without fuel can be fatal.

Talking to other pilots and getting their input on information on where to refuel is a big help. It is best to carry an extra can or two of fuel with you or at least a couple of empty cans so you can use those to put whatever kind of fuel available in. I have been forced to use regular automobile gas, or even some outboard motor gas mixed with oil. That makes it tough when you have a high performance engine like a 206 Cessna has. The engine strains for all its worth trying to get up enough power to climb over a mountain forcing me to take advantage of the air currents blowing up the face of the mountain in order to get enough altitude to clear the top.

Many times I have had to hitchhike a ride to some old abandoned airport to scrounge a few gallons of gas to get me out of a pinch. Flying a seaplane brings more of a challenge than a land plane. Learning to make the best approach on a river or small pond when certain wind conditions are present, such as crosswinds, downdrafts, updrafts, and especially glassy water is very important. It could save your neck.

With my home base being located on the south end of Lake Sunapee, New Hampshire, I had a ten-mile stretch of water to take off in. There were times when I needed every bit of that and then some. The altitude of Lake Sunapee is eleven hundred feet and on a calm day and ninety-five degrees, the 206 Cessna has to struggle with a heavy load. Of course, if I wasn't trying to carry the kitchen sink along with some big boys and their luggage it might not be so bad.

The altitude of the lake you are taking off from plays a big part in the takeoff performance of your aircraft. Having a good headwind will considerably reduce your takeoff distance. On the other hand, with little or no wind, with the same load, it will require a much greater distance for takeoff.

BUSH PILOTING
IN NEW ENGLAND

There is also a big difference in takeoff when the temperature is ninety degrees compared to fifty degrees. When the air is cold, the air is heavier and creats better lift. The hotter the air, the thinner it is, ultimately reducing the amount of lift or capability of carrying a bigger load.

On a beautiful fall day, under calm conditions, I like to jump in the seaplane at Lake Sunapee and head for northern New Hampshire. The first of October the foliage is at its peak and a sight to behold. Traveling by air has to be one of the best ways to enjoy the scenery.

As we fly north to the Connecticut River by way of Hanover, we follow the river over some of the richest farmland available to man. The mountains are glistening with all the brilliant colors of red, green, yellow and gold, especially from the sugar maple trees. It is easy to distinguish the difference between the maples and the deep blue green fur trees.

By October the rushing brooks of spring and summer have slowed down to just a trickle and the beaver dams scattered throughout the hills lay dormant. The joy of flying is filling our hearts with so much pleasure, it is hard to let go. Smarts Mountain passes us by on our right and off in the distance Sugar Hill and Cannon Mountain.

As the Connecticut River winds its way through the valleys and cornfields, we pass over the town of Orford and Haverhill. Mount Moosilouke with an elevation of forty-eight hundred and ten feet looms up off to our east as we leave the Connecticut River to pass over Lisbon and on to Littleton. From Littleton, we fly on to Whitefield and to Lancaster.

BUSH PILOTING
IN NEW ENGLAND

Far to the east, snow capped Mount Washington towers up to the height of six thousand two hundred and eighty feet. In Lancaster we again join up with the Connecticut River and follow it north to Colebrook and then on to the little town of Pittsburg. If you are flying in bad weather where you have to dodge in and out of the fog, it is very easy to cross over the Canadian border without realizing it, so I strongly suggest you watch your map closely.

Pittsburg is the home for many a sportsman. It is known for entertaining a lot of people on route three, a few miles north of town headed for the Canadian border. They call it moose alley, where people go and park beside the highway to sit in their lawn chairs and take pictures of the moose as they come out to feed beside the road.

Back Lake is located north of Pittsburg on the west side of Highway 3 and big enough to land a seaplane. The shoreline is dotted with cottages and is a great place for people to come and vacation. Years ago, Back Lake was known as a place that people can come and enjoy themselves and catch a few trout.

As we fly west over the hills, we come to Indian Stream nestled in a valley running all the way from the Canadian border. It used to be a hunter's paradise, but since logging took a priority it seems to have ruined the kind of hunting that hunters enjoy.

I have searched the waters of Indian Stream for that hard sought after gold, but could only come up with a few pieces hardly big enough to spot with a naked eye.

Many a stories have been told among the old cabins scattered along Indian Stream belonging to

BUSH PILOTING
IN NEW ENGLAND

trappers trying to make a living in furs and hunters looking for that trophy buck. How the Indians use to go into the village and trade their gold for goods. Even now I know of people still trying to strike it rich, but so far it has resulted in nothing but a dream.

"Dowsers" have had their brains picked, as well as topographic maps worn to a frazzel hoping to locate some of that shiny stuff called "gold." I have had my share of fun playing around this dowsing business, and actually have found some gold, but I don't see my pockets jingling yet.

If a person gets to be hungry, the local general store in Pittsburg serves a fine meal for the hearty. It also has a few gifts available for those wishing to take home a souvenir. Pittsburg may be a small village, but don't underestimate the people that live there. They come from all walks of life and from all around the country. There are those that know how to make a dollar, and maybe a few that don't care if they do. It's heaven for them.

One of the popular places to stay, is "Spruce Cone Lodge" on the edge of Lake Francis just north of town. Gary Bedell and his wife have owned and operated this lodge for quite a few years. I first got to know Gary when I flew him into Canada on a moose hunting trip. Gary knows his way around the Pittsburg area so anytime you have questions, stop in and see him. They cater to many sportsmen and snowmobilers.

Just north of Lake Francis are the First, Second, and Third Connecticut Lakes. The Third Connecticut Lake is next to the Canadian border. This area has been known also as a place for many sportsmen to get away from down below to come here and relax and do some fishing. It is a beautiful place to fly to for a day or two and just kick back.

Different times when I have flown over the Second Connecticut Lake I have seen salmon rising to the top of the surface, taking flies. This area also gives a few people a chance to view loons, for it is one of the loon's popular nesting places.

The reason why I am describing all this is to let the pilots know where to fly and what to expect if they want to get out of their own backyard. Spotting wildlife from the air is a lot fun, so have a good time.

After flying around the Pittsburg area we head east over the hill by the "Balsoms," a resort hotel and ski area. We then make our way through Dixville Notch and over to Errol. There is a small seaplane base on Akers Pond and an airport a couple of miles west of Errol.

The next leg of the trip we would follow the Androscoggin River south towards Berlin. Route 16 runs parallel to the river providing good access for the sportsmen for fishing and canoeing. Usually, moose can be seen feeding in the river while flying down it.

Depending on the weather, it makes a difference which side of Mount Washington you will want to fly. If the weather is good, you can cut through Franconia Notch, but beware of downdrafts. Otherwise, you can fly around to the east of Mount Washington that will take you over a much lower terrain and scattered lakes. I prefer flying this route when the weather is bad.

Trying to fly through rough mountain terrain in rain and heavy fog is no picnic. Once you get around the south end of Mount Washington you can cut across to Lake winnipasoukee and on to Lake Sunapee. This particular time of year a trip like I just mentioned is a very rewarding trip for pilots and his passengers. The foliage can be very beautiful, so bring your camera along.

Another enjoyable flight to take is flying to northern Maine and the Moosehead Lake area. Leaving from Lake Sunapee, New Hampshire, I would head easterly to Lake Winnipasoukee, then northeasterly to Conway, taking me just to the east of Mount Washington and over Mexico Maine.

Then, it would be a direct flight over Gadabout Gaddis airport just south of Wyman Dam by Bingham and on to Greenville Maine. The State of Maine has its share of moose. There are plenty of bogs and small ponds and beaver dams that provide the moose with nourishing food. It is quite common to see ten or twelve moose at one time gathered in one of these ponds feeding on lily pads and grass.

One bog in particular is just south of Greenville. I have seen some huge bull moose while flying over it. The best time of day to see moose is either early in the morning or late in the day. During mid day the moose generally find a safe haven back in the woods away from traffic to catch a little sleep. On rainy days they are most apt to be up and walking around.

Moosehead Lake is about forty-five miles long and has a lot of wilderness surrounding it. It also has a maze of logging roads around it providing access to the wilderness for many a sportsman.

There are several seaplane bases located on the south end of the lake in Greenville that give rides and fly people into their camps on remote lakes and ponds. They also supply fuel in case you run short.

People that wish to go on fire patrol with those that patrol the forest area by seaplane can do so. This gives a person plenty of opportunity to see wild game and enjoy the beautiful scenery.

The International Seaplane Fly-In held each year in September is a must see for pilots and people associated with flying. Just about any kind of floatplane flyable shows up at this show, including home built aircraft, experimental aircraft, DeHavilland Beavers, Grumman aircraft, Super Cubs, J-3s, and a variation of Cessna aircraft.

The highlight of one of the shows was a fly-by of Folsom's D C 3 on floats side by side with a Grumman Albatross. One unlucky pilot had the misfortune to overend his 172 Cessna in a gust of wind.

If you have the money, one type of aircraft that always stands out in my mind, is the 206 Cessna, of which I am very partial. It is one heck of a nice seaplane to fly and own.

After flying a 206 for twenty-eight years I think I can speak for how well it performs. I carried one big moose quartered, one smaller moose, baggage, and three of us all in one load. The next thing you have to be concerned with, is to make sure the lake is long enough to takeoff.

At the International Seaplane Fly-In, a variety of contests are conducted. Water bombing, transporting canoes, spot-landing contests, who can take off in the shortest distance, and a few more contests.

It is usually a three-day event with awards and dinner at night at one of the local lodges. I can only say, if you are in the area, it's a great time and event to take in.

Folsom's Air Service at the south end of Moosehead Lake is a good place to stop in and refuel. The family has owned and operated the seaplane base for many years. In fact, I had my first instructions at Folsoms when I first started flying a 206 Cessna.

Camping is allowed at the airport as well as plenty of parking available for those that attend the Fly-In.
It is quite a spectacle to walk around the airport at Greenville and look at all the different aircraft. Not only that, but it is very interesting chatting with the pilots that have come from Canada and many parts of the United States. I took a stroll over by some of the tents set up next to the owner's airplanes and got into a good exchange on some of their experiences and mine.

There always seems to be some wild story about someone surviving a crash or two, or maybe a hunting or fishing trip that didn't go like it was planned. Some of the pilots were gathered in a huddle trying to figure out how long it was going to take them to fly to a place in Canada. They got a ruler out and started measuring the flight map to check on the mileage to see how long it would take them to get to their destination.

As I stood there wondering what in the world was taking them so long to figure out a simple thing like that, I reached over and spread my hand over the chart and told them it would only take them a certain amount of time. My hand spread from thumb tip to my little fingertip is eight inches, so the flight map being eight miles to the inch represents sixty-four miles to each spread of my hand. This is the way I have measured my flying time for years and it gets me there within five minutes of my estimated time.

Getting away from talking about the International Fly-In, it's time to head north to Chesuncook Lake and on to Chamberlain Lake. Northern Maine has a vast amount of wilderness that supports a huge logging business. Lumber companies own most of the land and have gated off the access roads. If you are a hunter or fisherman it's nice to know someone in the lumber company to give you a key to one of the gates. Otherwise, forget it.

A flight around fifty-two hundred and sixty-seven foot high Mount Katadin is a spectacle in itself. A huge crater runs clear to the top rim of the mountain where years ago it appears the whole side of the mountain got blown out.

A few years back when I was flying in the area, I looked down into a shallow rocky bound lake and there sat an Aero Commander. It had run out of fuel and the pilot chose to land the aircraft among the rocks. I will say one thing, he did a good job of it. The wings were curled up a bit and a few other dings, but otherwise, not bad. Too bad he didn't have a set of floats under it. I believe they salvaged the aircraft with a helicopter.

The next stop was over to Shin Pond northeast of Mount Katadin. It may be only a whistle stop, but up the road a few hundred feet is a lodge where a person can get a bite to eat. There is a seaplane base next to the highway where you can refuel if your tanks are getting on the empty side.

BUSH PILOTING
IN NEW ENGLAND

Some of the sportsmen like to come here and do a little salmon fishing, or get flown into one of the lakes in the area for camping. Plenty of black bear and good deer hunting brings many a hunter to the region.

All in all, for someone who has a seaplane at his disposal, flying around northern Maine can be a lot of fun. Through rain, snow, or fog, or maybe if you are lucky to have a few good days, there is nothing like flying a seaplane. Maine can have its share of bad weather when old "Mother Nature" wants to kick up a storm.

The availability of seaplane bases in the State of Maine makes it convenient for pilots to fly just about anywhere in the state and not worry too much about having a place to refuel. From past experience, I have found the people to be hospitable and helpful in times of need.

One elderly lady that owned a lodge on Lake Millinocket put us up for three days. We made a deal with her that we would do her dishes and clean up things if she would give us a hand getting something to eat. I was on my way back home from a caribou hunting trip with some friends of mine and had to set down on Lake Millinocket because of weather. The heavy rain and fog was so bad we couldn't get out of Millinocket. She was even kind enough to let us use her old Cadillac to go into town to do some shopping.

Eventually, we were able to cut through the mountains and come onto Moose-head Lake and down to Greenville. From there, we flew back to New Hampshire.

So there you have it, a little touch of bush piloting in New England. I hope this will give you a general idea of what to expect when flying up here in the north woods. The love of flying with a little adventure thrown in for kicks will always bring a smile or two on the faces of a bush pilot and those that fly with him.

There is something to be said for flying in your own country, but when the call of the wild starts ringing in your ears, the only thing to take care of that is to jump in your seaplane and head north. It certainly beats sitting home watching television

ALASKA
ADVENTURES

In my first book titled "The Adventures of a Bush pilot," I take you from Lake Sunapee, New Hampshire to the Canadian border by a place called "The Thousand Islands" to clear Canadian Customs. From there I flew my 206 Cessna across Canada to British Columbia, the Yukon, and on to Anchorage, Alaska.

I had a flying job for a fishing lodge located on the Kvichak River by the Bering Sea that turned out to be quite an experience. At least I filled a long life's dream flying in Alaska and getting to see what the "Last Frontier" was all about.

People that have fled the lower United States for the adventure of living in Alaska have found it to be a style of living far removed from their past way of life. For one reason or another, some have returned to their individual states after many years in Alaska, but how I yearn to go back before I walk my last mile.

As life passes me by and I am getting closer to that last day, I think of the great time I had in Alaska, and my many adventures along the way. People are still amazed how I managed to survive all the ordeals dealt me throughout the years. How I struggled flying through snowstorms so thick I couldn't see my hand in front of me. Flying through what I call the killer fog that is so white and deadly. I guess the man upstairs was riding on my shoulders sheltering me from certain death, but thanks to him, I am still here and able to tell about my adventures.

When flying cross-country to Alaska, I found my new flight maps not too reliable concerning existing seaplane bases. A good share of them had been abandoned for many years, and yet, the people that made the maps failed to discard that information bringing the maps up to date. Pilots depend on this information and rely on it heavily, especially when it comes to needing fuel for their airplane.

Wilderness flying is quite a bit different than flying in civilization from airport to airport where fuel is readily available. Sometimes getting fuel in the wilderness of the northern woods is like trying to find a needle in a haystack. Seaplane bases are here, and gone tomorrow.

Scattered here and there tucked away in a quiet cove sits a drum of fuel next to some camp on a remote lake or pond. There have been times when luck was with me and I just happen to spot a seaplane landing on such a place, so down I would go. The pilot would oblige me by giving me enough fuel to get me to the next seaplane base.

They say, flying on air is okay if the propeller is turning, but if you run out of fuel the propeller won't be turning for very long. I know I like wilderness flying, but they never told me I had to push my luck trying to find fuel flying to Alaska.

It makes me wonder where all those missing aircraft are. Were they the victims of a search for fuel, not having quite enough fuel on board to make it to the next fuel stop. An aircraft can disappear into the bush and not be found for years, or maybe never.

ALASKA ADVENTURES

Squeezing in all the fuel to the point of overflowing wasn't always the best thing to do. When I happened to land on a lake two to three thousand feet above sea level, or higher, I have found myself in quite a predicament.

Fuel was running out of the overflow pipe and with the big load I had in the seaplane, when I climbed into the cockpit, I said, "wow, this baby is loaded to the hilt." All I had to do was to sit in my seat and I would get the feeling that the seaplane was overloaded. Before I was through trying to take off the lake, I ended up pumping some of that expensive fuel back out.

Why should I fly an airplane on wheels when I can have so much fun with a seaplane? My thoughts are, "escape to the north where all the lakes and rivers are, with its peace and tranquillity. Shall I satisfy that spirit of adventure and go and explore?"

Alaska was calling me for a long time, and as long as the opportunity knocked, why not take advantage of it. There is a different breed of people in Alaska. Once people from the lower states go to Alaska and get caught up in that type of life, it's hard to turn your nose back in the direction of south. They get caught up in the adventure and spirit of the "Last Frontier."

As I flew through the mountain passes and deep green valleys of British Columbia following mostly the Alaskan Highway, I was totally amazed with the scenery of snow-capped mountains, Glaciers, and many beautiful lakes.

High winds seem to be part of the normal problems with pilots when flying through British Columbia and into the Yukon. The tall mountains and big valleys seem to breed big winds. Pilots are always warned to

ALASKA
ADVENTURES

keep plenty of fuel on board in case they encounter big headwinds. Flight Service is on the radio telling you to make sure you have enough fuel to get you through to your next fuel stop.

When a pilot looses a lot of ground speed due to high headwinds, he can run out of fuel long before he gets to his destination. That's when a pilot is smart to make sure he allows for extra flying time, taking all these things into consideration.

Stopping at White Horse in the Yukon at a seaplane base on the river near the center of town gave me a chance to refuel the seaplane and grab a bite to eat. It also is a place for seaplanes to land and clear Canadian Customs flying back to the lower United States from Alaska.

Filing a flight plan from White Horse is a must when heading into Alaska. Flight Service just won't let you go unless you do. They keep pretty close tabs on pilots coming and going.

Next stop is Northway, Alaska. I had to give U.S. Customs advance notice of my arrival and contact flight control in Northway. Arrangements were made to have a Customs agent meet me at a lake just south of Northway.

I wasn't totally surprised to see the Customs agent arrive with a fellow in a pickup truck that brought me fuel for the seaplane. At this point in time, I had run into so many dealings while flying from New Hampshire, nothing would surprise me. I guess when you are flying in the wild, things have a tendency to follow the route of the unexplainable.

Northway had greeted us with double charging for Customs and the guy that brought the fuel. If that wasn't bad enough, the price of fuel took the cake. It was a good thing I had a friend of mine riding along with me to pay expenses.

The big deal was accommodations for the night and how we got from the lake to the Inn that must have been built back in the eighteen hundred gold rush days. I have done a lot of bush flying under all sorts of conditions, but let me tell you, when I am riding with a drunk driver down a twisty narrow road at ninety miles an hour, it's a different story.

With my fingers crossed under the seat and a few quiet prayers, the vehicle comes to a screeching halt in the yard of an old Inn. My friend and his wife aren't saying much, but the look on their face told the story.

Spending the night in an old rickety room with the door broken in and beds with a sag in them like the sway of an old mare's back wasn't the most comfortable situation. In the shadows of a dimly lit lounge sat several characters staring at us with beady eyes glistening in what little light there was.

It was a creepy feeling to say the least to be in a strange place not knowing whom I was dealing with. We had valuable items in the seaplane and I guess I spent all night worrying about that. The gal that owned the Inn was ready to go off the deep end. Her husband had taken off on a two weeks drunken binge in White Horse and left her to deal with running the place.

We managed to survive the night at the Inn, and come early morning made our way down the creaking stairway. I had made arrangements to hitch a ride to where we had the seaplane parked, but not with a drunken driver.

ALASKA
ADVENTURES

Late spring seems to bring a lot of bad weather. Flying from Northway to Anchorage old "Mother Nature" threw just about everything she could at us. I had to fly through more snowstorms, rain and fog than a pilot would normally see in five years. With the fog moving in and out of the hills and valleys so quickly, it was a hand full to deal with.

At times, the snow squalls were so heavy and thick, I didn't know if I could make it through to Anchorage. Flying through the mountain passes in this kind of weather was as treacherous as any pilot would want to do. Glaciers working their way down over the steep mountainsides were a spectacle to behold. It was an adventure to be sure.

When the visibility was good enough we were able to pick out several mountain goats and doll sheep grazing on the sides of the mountains. Occasionally, I would come upon a grizzly or two rambling through the thick brush near the shore of a lake or river. These critters are huge and nothing much can stop them once they get their mind set on something. I have had a few close encounters and wondered what I was doing trying to stare down a grizzly.

Grizzlies enjoy a nice piece of caribou when they can get their teeth into one, but their delicacy is a nice fat salmon. They especially enjoy it when they come into our camp and steal a fresh cooked king salmon. We have learned not to argue with these critters, but instead we step back at a good safe distance and let them go at it. Better safe than sorry, I say.

During the short summer months the grizzly has to put the food to him in order to store up enough fat to get him through the winter. After the mother grizzlies

ALASKA
ADVENTURES

have had their young they are very gaunt and have to do a lot of foraging to feed their young. It is unusual for a female grizzly to have four cubs, so you can imagine what a handful she has when that happens. At times, when I happen to be flying along the Kvichak River, I would look down and see four cubs frolicking with their mother. She was just laying there, letting them roll all over her.

Seeing all the wildlife and being able to get out into the wilderness watching "Mother Nature" at work is one of the biggest reasons why I like being a bush pilot.

Not far from Northway, the Wrangell Mountains tower up to an altitude of sixteen thousand three hundred and ninety feet. I wasn't about to play hero and fly over the tops of them without oxygen on board, let alone dealing with all the bad weather.

It was all I could do to fly at treetop or water level. Even the eagles didn't want to fly in all the snowstorms. The freezing rain probably would have frozen their eyes shut and they wouldn't have been able to see where they were going.

The terrain leveled out somewhat near Glennallen making the flight a little more enjoyable, but as I approached Palmer the weather went downhill again. It was especially tough when I flew by a mountain with a huge glacier. A heavy snow squall with wicked gusty winds gave me all I wanted to do to get through it. I had nowhere to go.

Backed up against one mountain on one side and another on my other raised my eyebrows a little. I was thinking, "boy, this is the wrong time of year to make this flight, either that, or "Mother Nature" just isn't co-

ALASKA
ADVENTURES

operating very much." It had become a time of decision making. Do I continue, or do I try and turn back.
Who knows, if I turned back, the weather could be
worse, and then I really would be in a pickle. A faint
heart never got anybody anywhere, so I figured the
best thing was to make my way toward Anchorage. It
wasn't that far away.

If I didn't like the kind of challenges flying as a bush
pilot brings, I wouldn't be here in the first place. I
would be sitting home in my rocking chair reading
about some other bush pilot and his adventures. But
look at all the fun I would miss. If I could keep my
nerves about me, and keep a cool head, I could
handle just about anything.

Well, I managed to get us through the bad stuff and
the town of Palmer, Alaska is just on our left. It has a
sizable airstrip next to town, and off to the south a
glacier winds its way through the rugged mountain
peaks into the valley below. Alaska is unique in that it
has so many valleys with rivers and lakes where so
many small towns have sprung up.

As I approached the eastern tip of Cook Inlet I ran
into a wall of fog that wouldn't quit. The nearest lake I
could land on was at Wasilla, a lake with many nooks
and crannies.

Almost every inch of shoreline had a camp or
house on it leaving me very few places to secure the
seaplane. Luckily, I was able to tie up to a dock belonging to a lodge and restaurant.

The weather had us socked in for a couple of days,
so we took that time and borrowed a vehicle to look
around the area and go into Anchorage. Anchorage
has many interesting shopping centers and other

ALASKA
ADVENTURES

points of interests. In the Malls there are many fascinating displays of mounted wildlife such as grizzlies, polar bears, goats, doll sheep and a variety of fish.

One of the popular fish that many people come to Alaska to catch is the king salmon. The largest I have heard of being caught was one hundred and twelve pounds. One of the rivers easily reached by vehicle and by boat is down on the Kenai. Camp grounds and guides are available in the area to ensure accommodations for the sportsmen.

During the months of June and July when the Kings are running, the grizzlies seem to know that by instinct. I have been kicked out of good fishing spots by the grizzlies so many times I can't count them.

Times when I have stood face to face with a grizzly, it's a guessing game of who is going to do what and when. Running away from one isn't going to do me any good, and standing there and arguing with one probably won't help either.

I had flown to a lake high in the mountains one day to see if I could find some arctic char and trout fishing. What a spooky feeling came over me when I noticed tons of bear tracks all over the beach and on the side hill overlooking the lake. God only gave me two eyes to see with, but this was one time I wish I had another set of eyes in the back of my head.

This happened to be one of the most beautiful places in the whole area. It was like a sportsman's dream come true. Scattered along the hillside were short, stubby spruce trees and on the ground lay a carpet of moss. Old dead logs dried to the weather from years of exposure lay along the shore of the lake.

ALASKA
ADVENTURES

Talk about purity in water. The water was so clear and pure looking, I could see the bottom of the lake like I was looking through a mirror. Arctic char could be seen swimming around as clear as day. It was so beautiful it made me want to build a log cabin there and stay for the rest of my days. So I say, "To heck with the rest of the world and its problems."

The problem with that idea about building the log cabin, the trees weren't big enough to withstand a few swipes of a bear's claws. Nothing in the cabin would be very safe from its reaches. There always seems to be a drawback in some bright idea.

For what short time we stayed on the lake, we had an enjoyable time of fishing. As far as lunch went, I didn't figure on attracting too many grizzlies so passed up cooking up some fish. I decided it might be better if we ate the packed lunch we had in the seaplane.

In the days to come, and with the fuel tanks chucked full, I flew across Cook Inlet towards the west to make my way through Lake Clark Pass. With glaciers on both sides of the pass and my camera clicking away, the inevitable happened. Just in front of me a mass of dark clouds obscures the horizon. The further I flew, the worse things became. The next thing I knew, I was down on the deck flying through another one of those miserable snowstorms.

Playing tag with the sides of mountains and glaciers was not exactly what I call fun. Lake Clark Pass is not very wide in some places so if the visibility got too bad and I had to do a one eighty to get away from a storm, I had to make sure I had the room to do it. I couldn't fly any lower than I was already and according to the flight map there was higher ground In front of me which would have put me up into the clouds. That's a no-no. No way am I going to get up where I can't see anything.

Finding the right spot to turn around and head back through the pass was a welcome sight, so while I had the chance I was heading back towards Anchorage.

About the only way to make it down by Bristol Bay was to fly along Cook Inlet and cut through another mountain pass, down onto Lake Illiamna, and from there I was flying water level over the Kvichak River to my destination.

Once in a while a bush pilot has to have some kind of bad weather to fly in to help keep him sharp. I know my life as a bush pilot, has been anything but dull.

Flying sportsmen for so many years, I have gotten to know a lot of different people. There are many different personalities. There are those that I call characters, and some I don't care to mention, like the ones I don't care to fly again. Some are rich, and then we have the working person that knows how to enjoy a trip.

There are no two people alike, unless you are perfect twins. Everyone has his own quirks and ideas. But for the most part, I have really enjoyed the people I have flown. Maybe I have the gift of gab to get along with most people. When I get in a pinch flying, and things get a little tight, that's when I really get to know the person I am flying. You know how it is, your palm gets to sweating, and the sweat starts running off your forehead. You reach down and tighten up the seat belt another notch. Then you start looking around and wonder what you can do to survive the ordeal. Maybe, if you grab the controls, you take over flying the airplane and get rid of the guy on your left. But you don't really know how to fly the airplane. In the mean time, the sweat keeps coming. The one easy way to handle all of the pressure is to shut your mouth, sit back and let the pilot do the flying. "Okay?'

It is always an adventure exploring new territory. I can look at a flight map and it can tell me where the mountains are, the lakes and the rivers, but it's the unknown that sneaks up on me and bites me in the rear. It has happened to me a few times.

It may have been a situation where I hadn't been in a particular remote outpost for a year. This was a place where they had an airport, a seaplane base, a motel, and a trading post. It was a small settlement out in the wilderness that housed a few sportsmen and minors. What used to be a hopping little settlement is no longer.

The mining company had shut down its operation as well as the settlement. When I next flew there to refuel and purchase a few groceries, to my surprise, there were no buildings left standing. Nothing but empty cement slabs where the buildings sat.

The whole town had been leveled by bulldozers, leaving nothing but a ghost town. I was low on fuel and heaven knows where I was going to get some. As far as food supplies go, I would have to fly to another town far to the east. That is, if I could find the fuel to take me there.

In the past, I could remember a fishing camp on a small lake south of me. My only hope was to go there and just maybe I could find enough fuel to get me to a seaplane base. I didn't care if it was outboard motor gas mixed with oil, or what. As it turned out, I was able to find fuel and get me out of a bad situation.

Being a bush pilot has its share of ups and downs, and it's nice that my life is not so boring. I have to mark on my flight map different changes that take place over time and the places I can get fuel in case of an emergency. I can't very well get on the phone and call up somebody to bring me fuel or supplies.

Flying in the area near the Bering Sea is always a challenge when it comes to bad weather. The moisture off the ocean tends to help create more stormy weather. Fog banks move onto shore to make some pretty tough flying conditions for pilots that want to fly into some of the fishing villages.

At times, the only way I have been able to navigate the bad weather was to fly at ground level over the tundra, or sneak down a river into Bristol Bay and then up the Naknek River to the town of King Salmon. Because of so many commercial fishing boats going up and down the river it kept me busy dodging the boats while I was flying so low over the river.

Finding a place to tie up at one of the local docks was another problem. The competition between the boats and all the activity of seaplanes coming and going at the docks kept me on the alert. Sometimes, it was a case of taxiing around in the river waiting for a seaplane or boat to leave the dock, and I would rush in a grab the spot before someone else gets it.

The town of King Salmon is a busy little place. Several commercial airlines occupy the one airport along with the United States Air Force and its fighter planes. I have often stood by the docks and watched the fighter planes take off and head straight up into the sky and wished I had that power in my 206 Cessna. I wouldn't have to be concerned so much when I take off from those very small beaver dams on some mountainside.

My job flying for a fishing lodge on the Kvichak River was to fly into King Salmon to pick up their clients along with all their baggage, food supplies and other necessities. One time I even had to squeeze in a power generator and fly that back to the lodge.

During their weeks stay I would fly them to remote rivers and lakes fishing for salmon and rainbow trout. My profession as a pilot and guide was very interesting to say the least. I got to know people from all walks of life and even learned a little about their different cultures.

I have come to know one thing, and that is when a person spends the big bucks to make a trip to Alaska for fishing or hunting, he wants a full week of it. These sportsmen keep us bush pilots hopping and not much time to rest. I suppose the summer season being so short puts pressure on the lodges to make their money while they can.

Things are pretty well figured out and schedules made to take them through the season. Depending on how well the lodges treat their help normally tells how long the help will hang around. That includes the bush pilots they hire. The same goes for the commercial fishing boats when they hire on the college kids. The young boys and girls read about all the jobs on the fishing boats and once they get there, they find out its not what it is was cracked up to be.

Going to Alaska has been the dream of many people. Some like it very much and some find out it is not for them. I will say, it is an experience that you can't learn out of a book.

When I think back a few years, the sight of the beautiful scenery of Alaska and its mountains and lakes flash through my mind, I wish I had known about my capability to dowse for gold. Maybe it was ESP, but there were a few times when my gut told me, "there has to be gold in those hills." I would have picked up a few friends of mine and spent a summer dowsing for gold.

Having the seaplane would have made it much easier to get around to the remote areas. I didn't realize I could dowse for gold, as well as a lot of other things, until a couple of years after I was in Alaska. Perhaps God willing, I will have another chance at it.

Living in pretty much their own traditional way of life, the Eskimos continue dealing with the ever increasing amount of boats and airplanes. When I am flying along the different rivers, lakes, and bays, I look down on the Eskimo villages scattered along the shores.

Fish drying racks full of salmon was a common thing to see. The Eskimos stock up a good supply of fish to get them through the winter months. They manage to pull in some extra money by using barges to deliver supplies and fuel to the different lodges along the waterfront.

Flying out for a day of fishing usually turned out to be a lot fun. Getting an early start shortly after a good hearty breakfast was the order for the day. Giving my seaplane a close checkup before taking off was a must. Checking the engine oil and topping off the fuel tanks was most important.

ALASKA
ADVENTURES

Every time I flew anybody out for the day, I made sure each person had his sleeping bag and we had a tent and other survival equipment in the seaplane. This is a safety precaution in case we got stuck in bad weather, or engine problems.

Having engine trouble was the least of my concerns only because I was very careful taking good care of the engine myself. I didn't trust other mechanics as far as I could throw them. I can name several cases where I almost bit the dust, but for the knowledge I possessed. Things like losing all of the engine oil on takeoff, or having the engine seize tighter than a drum just before I was ready to take off on a dolly at an airport being towed by a vehicle. All caused by so-called licensed mechanics.

I don't want to spoil the fun so we had better get going. Flying off the Kvichak River, we headed north west across open tundra. Surprisingly, there were very few lakes or bodies of water over a stretch of tundra about one hundred miles long.

The weather was actually pretty decent and would stay that way for the rest of the day. It gave us a chance to do our thing flying here and there without the hassle of fighting the elements. Off to our west the waters of the Bering Sea glistened in the early morning sun as if to say, "have a nice day and good fishing."

We were up to looking for some new fishing holes, and ahead of us ran the Nushagak River. It empties into Nushagak Bay by Dillingham. From the mouth of the river upstream a few miles the river is controlled by the tide. After making a few passes over the river I managed to find a beach to pull up to without getting into a bunch of rocks. No sooner had we tied the seaplane down and got out the fishing rods we heard a wicked big splash out in the river. It sounded just like someone had hit the water with a big paddle. "Kbam."

For someone that had never fished for king salmon before, this definitely was quite an experience. Some of the fellows fished with fly rods and those that wanted to get the action in a hurry, I put them on a sack of salmon eggs attached to a hook. It didn't take long to hear the sound, "Zzzzzzz" when a king salmon hit the line and headed for the ocean.

The king salmon has a huge tail and knows how to use it. It can travel quite a distance in a short time, and when it comes to surface, that big tail drives it into the air with such force, the guy on the other end of the rod has to really hang on.

By the time the fish gets through running up and down the river, the guy holding the rod is having a hard time holding his arms up. The way I see it, a guy had better do some tall working out to get him in shape for dealing with these salmon.

We were catching salmon up to eighty pounds, but many were in the forty to sixty pound range. We were all so busy catching fish, nobody was paying much attention to the water level. Having a nice stretch of dry ground to stand on while you're fishing makes it handy. My seaplane was pulled up to that piece of dry ground, but in a matter of minutes, it was floating up in by the bushes overhanging the river.

The guys fishing were backed up to the bushes with the water up to the top of their hip boots. The salmon were hitting fast and furious, but I had to scramble over to my seaplane and secure it in such a way that the bushes overhanging the river wouldn't damage the wings or tail section. Being the pilot and owner of my seaplane, it's my responsibility to make sure it stays in good condition to get us back to the lodge or into civilization.

As time passed and the salmon continued to give us a battle royal, I noticed we had been inching our way out toward the center of the river not realizing the tide was on its way out. When I turned to check on how my 206 was doing, I saw that it was sitting high and dry on bare ground. I should have been keeping a closer eye on it considering the tide was moving the level of water down and out to sea. A seaplane weighing about twenty-five hundred pounds is no easy task to shove off from bare ground.

After a lot of heaving and tugging, the gang finally was able to help me get the seaplane into deep water. This incident wasn't quite so bad as the time I overshot my landing strip in a small lake with glassy water.

While taking off, the crosswind conditions were so strong and accompanied by up and down drafts, I was forced to set the seaplane back down onto the end of the lake in order to keep from crashing into the trees.

Landing on glassy water is like landing on a slick batch of ice and with a heavy load and not any room to spare, things can get pretty hairy. About the only thing left to do was to cross my fingers and pray. After that episode, I sometimes think I should start carrying an anchor to throw out to slow the seaplane down when I need to.

There was no stopping the seaplane, it slid along the water like it was gaining speed instead of slowing down. It eventually came to a halt about twenty feet on the soggy grass in the swamp at the end of the lake. We had to cut several large poles to use as pries to lift and tug on the seaplane to get it back into the lake.

There have been times in my career as a bush pilot, and I may add other times in my life, that making the right and quick decision has made a difference in my survival. Perhaps, if I weren't always in the adventurous mood, I wouldn't be getting into all those predicaments.

When the wrong conditions exist, you have to do the next best thing. That is to unload some of that extra weight and fly what you have to a larger lake. Then go back to get the rest of what you left on the small lake. These are some of the consequences of flying into a small beaver dam or small body of water just to have a little extra fun.

Getting back to my story on catching one of the fightingest fish I have hooked onto. There is probably nothing any more delicious than sinking your teeth into a freshly caught king salmon fillet. Especially when its cooked over an open fire next to the river's edge wrapped in tinfoil with some butter and a little seasoning and lemon.

With the tide out, at least we didn't have to worry about our salmon steaks being washed out to sea. The only other thing that could have happened, it wouldn't have surprised me a bit to see the thick bushes on the shore of the river parting company and see a huge brown object coming at us. Grizzly bears just love eating fresh cooked salmon.

After a long happy day on the river catching salmon, we couldn't wait to get back to camp and plan for another day of fishing. It's always nice to see a smile on a client's face after a day of fishing. When the fish aren't biting well, the expression changes to a long, gloomy look of dissatisfaction wondering where did all the fish go. Just "Mother Nature" at work again.

I hadn't gotten familiar with the habits of some of the other bush pilots in Alaska yet, but I was learning. It's like "dog eat dog" when it comes to flying into a chosen hotspot on a river.

The following day, I flew some fellows to the upper reaches of the Nushagak River. There was about twelve seaplanes circling the area as though they were looking over the river to decide where to land.

One of my guys leans over and taps me on the shoulder and says, "Richard, first come, first serve, that's the way they do it here." He didn't have to tell me twice. I peeled off with the seaplane and dove for a turn in the river where I could see it should be a good fishing spot. I guess I had picked a spot the other pilots wanted to take, they kind of circled over our head after I landed and continued on.

How little did the sports know how much flying into small places I had done. There wasn't much that got by me when it came to fishing and hunting and being able to pick out the good places. My years of experience taught me a few things.

As I pulled towards shore near a bend in the river, the strong current striking hard against the floats made it difficult to pull up to the bank. Someone had to jump ashore with a rope and anchor the seaplane to the nearest bush. This is when someone usually falls off the float into the river, or maybe the man with the rope gets a little nervous scrambling to do the right thing and can't get the job done. The next thing I know, the seaplane is floating down the river headed for some rocks and I have to get the engine started in a hurry. Then I have to give the right act to the man with the rope and tell him just how it has to be done. It's all in good fun.

As soon as I finally managed to get the seaplane tied safely to shore, out came the fishing rods. One of the fellows had come all the way from New Hampshire to catch one king salmon. He hadn't been having much luck, so I offered to put a batch of salmon eggs on his hook and a bobber on his line. I explained to him, "If you throw the line out and see your bobber disappear, set the hook, but good. The salmon have a tough jaw."

He didn't have to wait long before his bobber was out of sight. A huge king salmon had grabbed his line and went down the river headed for the ocean. For over an hour I was busy talking to the man at the end of the fishing rod telling him just what to do to land the fish. He was sweating cobs like you wouldn't believe. I asked him, "who's winning the battle, you or the fish?" He says, "I think the fish is."

He managed to get the fish almost to shore and it would take off down the river, again and again. I had to take his jacket off, then his vest to cool him down some, but I could see he was just about done in. I didn't know he had a heart condition and I don't if he knew himself.

After an hour and fifteen minutes passed, he finally got the fish up to the shore. I grabbed a club from a beaver dam and hit the salmon over the head and finally got it under control. Moments later, I asked the person if he would like to try for another salmon. I guess he was plumb tuckered out, because he told me, "Richard, my purpose of coming to Alaska was to catch just one of these critters, thank you for your help, I don't think I can handle another one." When he arrived back home in New Hampshire, a short time later, he died of a heart attack.

The salmon were traveling up the river in a deep channel carved out by the strong current making its way through the bend in the river. Everyone was hooking into salmon with almost every cast. When a salmon cleared the water it would make such a huge splash and swirl, it was as though someone had dropped a big rock from a hundred feet up.

When the salmon first leave the ocean and return to the river where they were spawned, they are very silver in color. After a week or two in the river, as they too near their spawning time, they change from silver to reddish brown, greenish and a little yellowish. Their jaws become hooked to a large degree. It's like the fish goes through a period of deformation before it dies.

Most of the salmon will die after spawning and in turn become easy prey for the eagles and bear. One of "Mother Nature's" ways of keeping the food chain going, and fattening up the bear for the long hard winter. I cannot emphasize how much I wish everyone could see the wonders of Alaska.

As much as I have flown around the North Country, I still enjoy seeing pictures of Alaska and northern Canada. Every time I show my slides to different organizations and tell them about my adventures, it makes me want to jump in a seaplane and head north. I suppose that will be until the day I die.

To a sportsman, it is quite an asset to be in the company of a bush pilot who is also a good guide, but most importantly he be a person with a lot of sixth-sense. Better yet, it is nice he is able to detect good fishing areas, along with having the sense to know where the good hunting spots are. It's like I was given this gift to pass on to other generations.

The salmon were right in the middle of their spawning run up the river. As long as they kept coming, we kept catching fish. It got to the point where the guys decided to take it easy. Some sat around and joked, while some continued fishing. When it came time to eat, everyone was happy to take a break and down some of that delicious salmon.

That one hotspot had given the guys so much action I didn't have to break my back convincing them it was time to head back to lodge. All they could talk about on the way back was how I dove the seaplane down onto the river cutting off a dozen other seaplanes to take charge of a great fishing hole. Of course, what else could they talk about, but all the good fishing they had that day.

On another day, it was my job to fly a German fellow to explore for more fishing spots. The lodge I was working for had to make sure we had plenty of places to fly the clients. Rotating the fishing spots kept the clients interested and more excited when they didn't have to go to the same old places time and time again.

The owner of the lodge figured it would give me a change in pace as well, and if anyone could find another hotspot, it was me. I had been studying my flight map looking over another section of river upstream from an Eskimo village northeast of Dillingham. The German fellow seemed quite excited to have the opportunity to be the only one to fly with me without having a gang of four in the seaplane.

Flying north, following the zigzags and twisty turns of the Nushagak at one hundred feet over the river was a lot of fun. An occasional glance at the eyes of my passenger told me he was deeply engrossed at the scenery, but in particular, he seemed more interested in looking down at the river for a good place to fish.

As we came to a bend in the river, I noticed hundreds of king salmon swimming along the inside bend of the river next to shore. As my German friend's eyes focused on all those beautiful salmon, his eyes lit up like a five-thousand-watt bulb.

A quick fly around to check for rocks or logs in the river and down we went. Due to the strong current in the river I had to power the seaplane nose first upon the bank of the river.

After making sure the seaplane was secured to a bush on shore I stepped toward the rear of the floats to see if I could see any salmon. I saw salmon by the hundreds. There were salmon of all sizes swimming under the tail section of my seaplane.

It seemed funny to be standing on the floats, dangling a fly under the seaplane and see a huge salmon grab the fly and head downstream with so much ferocity. Even with a spinner on the end of my line, all I had to do was to jiggle it in the foot or two of water and a salmon would grab it.

ALASKA
ADVENTURES

The German fellow had about two hundred yards of regular fly line and three hundred yards of backing, but do you think he could haul that fish in. No way, the salmon stripped his reel clean. There stood a mighty disgruntled fisherman. I don't know how to swear in German, but he was going at it like a trooper.

I had managed to catch a few decent sized salmon with my little brook trout fishing rod with twelve-pound test line on my Zepco spinning reel. Seeing a little smoke rise from my reel told me I needed to have a heavier duty reel to handle this kind of fishing.

With no extra fishing gear, my German fishing companion decided to call it quits. He said, "take me back to the lodge." Our day was considerably shortened. This was a man that gathered together a group of sports from Germany, bringing them to Alaska for salmon fishing. I think if I was flying out for a day of fishing I would have brought some extra gear along. Maybe he had so much confidence in his fly rod, he didn't figure he needed anything more.

Hooking into a salmon weighing in the range of fifty to eighty pounds is going to give anybody a handful, no matter what they have for gear. To me, the fun of just being out there and flying around the countryside is reward enough. How many people would really be in their glory if only they had the chance to do what I have had the pleasure of doing for so many years.

A salmon just doesn't come up and nibble at your line, he grabs it with the idea it's his, and off he goes come hell or high water. The energy that a salmon releases under these conditions is tremendous. That big tail of his can get him around in a hurry and with plenty of strength. I guess that's what makes it so much fun fishing for salmon.

Not all days go by without a few thrills. On a day I flew some sports to fish in the Katmai National Park, we had all kinds of excitement. I parked the seaplane at the mouth of the river near the lodge hoping to enjoy a few hours of fishing for salmon and rainbow trout. What I didn't realize, was the four-foot wide trails running along the river were grizzly trails, and not human trails. The further up the river we went, the more bear sign.

Telling a grizzly to move over and let you take over that part of the river so you can do some fishing, just doesn't work very well. They either don't understand English, or we can't talk bear talk.

When we got to a certain part of the river, there were several grizzlies chasing some salmon around the shallow waters. I figured it was best not to argue with them as they had us outnumbered. Besides, I really didn't want to provide a meal for them.

We quietly circled around them without stirring up too much commotion, but to our surprise, a big old grizzly had moseyed over behind a brush pile and when we came along, he decided to show his teeth to us. Standing on his hind feet about ten feet tall with its jaw wide open and claws bared didn't exactly give us a comforting feeling.

For a few frantic minutes, we were undecided as to what to do. I always thought the best thing to do was not to excite a bear, play it cool and see what it wants to do. Maybe he isn't so hungry after all. Retreat slowly and hope he doesn't charge.

ALASKA
ADVENTURES

The people with me didn't take time to think. They went running and screaming down the river and left me standing there alone. I was concerned that the grizzly would get frustrated with all the noise so I tried to convince them to come back to me. As they made their way close to where I was standing, the grizzly dropped down onto all fours and made his way onto the river. I guess he preferred salmon to us.

Black bear can be very dangerous as well. I have had plenty of close encounters with them. It is a telltale sign when the hair on the neck of a bear stands straight up. That is a warning to get out of its way, especially if a mother bear has young with her. There have been many people surprised in a berry patch because bears love berries.

Wherever we went that day in the Katmai National Park, we kept running into grizzlies. It's like we needed eyes in the back of our head. We did manage to get in some fishing, but it was mostly a picture taking day.

During my stay in Alaska, things went pretty much like what I have told you. Doing a lot of treetop flying, or flying low over the tundra and along the rivers in order to get to where I needed to go.

Dodging snowstorms and flying through rain and fog were pretty much an every day routine. Keeping a cool head and watching my flight maps closely while in strange territory got me through the bad times.

I had my own business in northern Quebec to take care of, and my stay in Alaska was winding down. People that have read my first book, "The Adventures of a Bush Pilot," have asked me about any problems I may have had flying back home to New Hampshire.

ALASKA
ADVENTURES

The day had come for my departure from a very busy schedule of flying and guiding fishermen at "No See Um Lodge" on the Kvichak River. A very good friend of mine by the name of Bill Ljungren had flown by commercial air from Massachussetts to King Salmon just to fly back to New Hampshire with me. I had gotten to know him from previous years when I flew he and his wife to northern Quebec fishing for speckled trout.

After refueling the seaplane and saying our goodbyes, the long flight to New Hampshire got under way. My flight through Lake Clark Pass became impossible due to very bad weather. I was forced to fly east of Lake Illiamna through Bruin Pass at ground level over open tundra.

With mountains on my left and a valley below, rain and fog persisted to the point of being so difficult to fly through I was almost ready to do a one-eighty and go back to the lodge. I couldn't afford to waste the fuel I had on board so figured I should try and continue on. There were a few lakes I could land on if need be.

Bruin Pass is known to have its share of grizzlies. That's where it got its name. At different times, I was flying so low in order to see through the fog when I came upon a grizzly I had to actually fly around it to avoid hitting it. It would be suicide to climb higher and get into the clouds where I wouldn't be able to see. Crashing into a mountain was not my cup of tea.

Fortunately, I managed to get through Bruin Pass and over to Cook Inlet and on towards Anchorage. The wind had picked up to a strong gale sweeping across the large body of water and causing huge waves.

ALASKA
ADVENTURES

As if I hadn't had enough trouble flying through such rough conditions, having to fly at water level and dealing with huge whitecaps added to my problems. I made radio contact with the airport in Anchorage and was told the weather was okay there, so I could relax a little knowing at least the closer I got to Anchorage, the better the weather would be.

Flying along the north shore of Cook Inlet was a little on the tough side due to the big winds, but I was watching my flight map closely picking out the different bays I could duck into in case the storm got worse. With luck on our side we managed to get to Anchorage. We would spend one night there and get rested up for a long flight the following day.

I have flown through some pretty tough weather in the past, but the trip from the lodge to Anchorage was about as rough as any pilot would want to deal with.

Believe it or not, we actually had a beautiful day when we departed Anchorage the following morning. I made sure I topped my fuel tanks off to make sure I would have enough fuel to get us into White Horse in the Yukon. I had to file a flight plan to keep the control tower happy, so when we arrived in White Horse the Canadian Customs wouldn't chew us out.

Because of so many high mountains and deep valleys it tends to breed what I call wicked, big and powerful winds. After a few days of bad weather, it usually takes some pretty powerful winds to clear the air. Well, that is exactly what happened.

We had good conditions until we hit Northway, Alaska, but shortly after that we ran into the strongest headwinds. Northway control kept bugging me on the radio telling me to turn around and stop to refuel. An hour later, they were still calling me telling me I wouldn't make it into White Horse because of the strong headwinds. I suppose they knew what they were talking about as they had plenty of experience dealing with first time pilots flying through their area. I kept telling them I was okay, and thanks very much for their concern.

The further I flew, the more I realized how right they were in telling me to take on some extra fuel. I kept watching the fuel gauge go down while calculating my flying time to White Horse. Bucking the strong headwinds were gobbling up my fuel, and to be on the safe side I started looking for a place to land.

I had been advised by the Canadian Customs that once I file a flight plan I was not allowed to stop anywhere between a scheduled flight. Well, I got to tell you, if it's a case of saving my neck, nobody is going to keep me from stopping if I am being faced with running out of fuel. I'd rather get chewed out than to be a statistic rapped around some mountainside.

It was my luck to spot a seaplane coming in for a landing on a small lake, so I wasted no time following him down. The pilot was good enough to sell me a few gallons of fuel to ensure I would have enough to get us into White Horse.

The Canadian Customs agent was waiting patiently for me to arrive and asked that question. "Did you by any chance stop along the way?" "It took you longer for some reason." I told him, "Gee, those head-winds were some strong. It really slowed me down." I don't know if he believed me, or not.

Knowing we had a long flight to our next stop, I figured it was best to put up in a motel in White Horse.

ALASKA
ADVENTURES

We had plenty of daylight hours to make a longer day of it later.

From White Horse I flew the shortest route possible through some of the mountain passes and on to Fort St. John, British Columbia. I found it easier to follow the Alaskan Highway when possible, but to save time I took advantage of flying through some of the mountain passes.

Lake Charlie was one of my scheduled fuel stops on my way to Alaska. There were very few places to refuel east of there, making it imperative we stop at Lake Charlie. If you read my first book, you probably read about all the troubles I had trying to take off in the early morning hours.

With no wind, glassy water, and a huge load on board, it took me about two hours before I was able to take off. As the morning hours crept by, finally, a little gust of wind kicked up on a section of the lake. It was only then that I was able to take advantage of what little wind there was, so I headed the seaplane towards it.

Just as I got to it, I pulled back on the controls and managed to pop the seaplane into the air. I would have had no problem if the altitude of the lake were at sea level, but instead, it was at twenty-six hundred and eighty feet above sea level. The higher the lake in altitude, the thinner the air becomes, making a big difference in the amount of weight one can carry in his airplane.

It was still early in the day when we stopped at Lake Charlie to refuel, so we didn't waste much time heading out on the next leg east. With only one other person in the seaplane, it was a pleasure to fly the

206 Cessna. Instead of carrying empty fuel cans aboard, I was able to carry them full in case we ran low, giving me a feeling of assurance when flying across the long stretches of desolate wilderness.

Other than one large lake and a few rivers, the territory between Fort St. John, British Columbia and Edmonton, Alberta was about as desolate as a person would want. Flying seven or eight hundred miles over nothing but prairies and wooded land put the thought in my head, hoping I wouldn't have engine problems. It could be a rough landing if I had to land out in the sticks somewhere.

Our next fuel stop was supposed to be at Lac La Biche just north of Edmonton. Once again, there was no fuel available. We had to fly south a few miles to a small lake where a fellow had his own private seaplane base.

It seemed every time I stopped at a place where there was supposed to be a seaplane base, that is according to my flight maps, it no longer existed. I would have to take off and go search for fuel in some other area. Sometimes, it was a case where I had to depend on some drunk driver to transport me by vehicle. I think that was the most dangerous part of my whole trip.

By now, we had flown about two thousand miles since leaving Anchorage. We were fortunate to have good weather and made better time flying east due to a good tail wind. I thought it was quite a surprise to actually have things working in our favor for a change.

Flying at lower altitudes gave us a chance to see all kinds of wildlife. We were able to spot moose feeding in the area of beaver dams, and deer and elk scattered here and there through the countryside. We even had the pleasure of seeing trout rising to the surface of an occasional small pond leaving that familiar circle on the water of a fish jumping to take a fly that dare venture too close.

I guess the highlight of the trip back to New Hampshire was when we arrived in Saskatoon, Saskatchewan. The long arm of the "Law" showed its authority when I pulled up to a beautiful beach beside town. Now, I have to tell you again, I swear by the scout's honor, my flight map shows a seaplane base should be where I landed. I thought it strange that there were no seaplanes around.

Within a couple of minutes of me pulling up to shore, I was surrounded by Canadian Mounted Police and Fish and Game Wardens. They had already started writing me up in their summons book, writing down the tail number of my aircraft, type, and so on.

I had quite a time defending myself, and had to get out my flight map to prove my case. Darkness was closing in on us as we spoke and my biggest concern was to have a safe place to keep the seaplane overnight.

It's like all my pleas were falling on deaf ears. The "Law" says, "Move your seaplane immediately, or we will impound it and take you off to jail. It is against the "Law" to land here, let alone to park your seaplane here." I said, "But officer, you don't understand, I just don't go flying off into the dark of the night to some strange place I have never flown before. What if I hit a rock or log sticking up in the water."

Well, if you have ever argued with the "Law" you can understand how frustrated I became. Right or wrong, they insisted I fly my seaplane out of there, and immediately. So........up in the dark of night I go, headed south about seventy miles to a Forest Ranger Station I had never been to before.

I was angry to say the least. To think the "Law" acted in such a way, and put my life and my friend at risk and possibly death. What happened to common sense? Being forced to fly at night by instrument with a seaplane in unfamiliar territory was bad news.

Luckily, between using my ADF (Automatic Directional Finder) and my navigational frequencies working off two VOR stations I was able to locate the area of the Ranger Station on a lake. It was difficult making out the shoreline of the lake. All I could see looking down was a dark outline of a lake. If there were any islands or rocks, I could not see them.

As I dropped altitude to line up on the lake, the scary thoughts of hitting a rock entered my mind, or what if I overshot the lake. Maybe once I landed, I wouldn't be able to get stopped in time before I hit the trees on the end of the lake. There are plenty of things to think about under these kinds of conditions.

Slowly, but slowly, I set the seaplane down onto the lake, hoping I wouldn't collide with a boat full of people, or whatever. One night in Quebec, Canada, flying back from the north in pitch black, I was slipping down over the side of a mountain just missing the treetops making an approach on a lake, I touched down and got stopped right beside two lovers in a boat. I am sure they had the surprise of their life.

To make the story short, I landed safely and taxied through the darkness to find the Ranger Station. The Rangers couldn't believe what I told them had happened, and were good enough to let us borrow a vehicle to find a motel for the night. They didn't know how much to charge me for the fuel and said they would send me a bill. Several months later, I finally recieved the bill.

Flying the rest of the way home to New Hampshire was pretty much uneventful except when we got over Vermont, I had to set down on a lake near a set of cottages. "Mother Nature" decided to show her wrath once again. Heavy rain and fog was too much for me to handle around the mountains. So close, and yet so far away from home. Forty-five minutes would have put us in our own back yard on Lake Sunapee.

While we were hanging around the dock on a lake near Rutland, Vermont, I got talking with a young fellow on vacation. I thought I would have a few laughs. I had brought back a bag of puma stone that I picked up from a lake in the Katmai National Park in Alaska. When I landed there on a lake, I actually had several pieces of puma stone sitting on the top of my floats. I had no idea how that came about, but after-wards, I realized they had come from one of the volcanoes that had erupted shortly before I arrived in Alaska.

Realizing that puma stones float, I jokingly told the young fellow that I would bet him twenty-five dollars I could make my rock float and that he couldn't make the rock float that I picked out of the lake in Vermont and gave him. I guess he hadn't heard much about puma stone being able to float, but I figured a joke is a joke, and I laughingly gave him back his money.

The following day brought the climax to a great summer of flying in Alaska. The weather had cleared enough to get through the mountains and home to

ALASKA
ADVENTURES

Lake Sunapee, New Hampshire. I can only say, it took a good friend to come all the way to Alaska just to turn around and fly back with me. He since has passed on to a better place and I hope he reads my book one day. I have enjoyed quite a few excellent fishing trips with he and his wife in northern Quebec catching those beautiful trophy speckled brook trout.

They especially enjoyed roughing it, camping out on some remote lake near the mouth of a river, handy to make a few casts. A few days of relaxing and watching "Mother Nature" do her thing is what makes it all worthwhile.

THE WOES
OF MOOSE HUNTING

Each year, the month of October rolls around. In the province of Quebec, Canada, it marks the coming of moose season. The seaplane bases have already been busy hustling the hunters back into the bush with all their baggage, liquor, some food, and those things they call guns. The guns are supposed to be the weapon to shoot the moose with, if the hunter is fortunate enough to see a moose to shoot at.

Occasionally, the gun is used to shoot a hunter, by mistake of course. Families become distraught, loved ones are lost, or maybe the hunter that gets shot is just wounded and survives, but will live with that horrible memory forever.

It's strange, the human mind, how it works when there is so much anxiety when a hunter prepares for his trip to the bush. I often stand around the seaplane bases watching the different people gather at the dock to load their supplies into the seaplane. I study their faces and wonder, what kind of people they are. Some have weather-beaten faces, and some with smooth baby faces. Perhaps some of them have a desk job where they don't get out in the wilderness much.

One thing for sure, they are all there to go hunting for the moose. Once in a while one of the hunters may get lucky and shoot a bear while he is on his hunting trip.

THE WOES
OF MOOSE HUNTING

As each group of moose hunters with their heavily loaded seaplane taxi down to the very end of the lake for that long hard takeoff, their anxiety starts building. All they can hope is that they are able to clear the mountain at the other end of the lake. They pear out the cockpit window to see if their canoe is safely secured to the floats.

There have many times where I have heard of canoes coming loose and falling off the seaplane and tumbling down through the air into the forest below. That explains why sometimes I have seen a canoe hung up in some tree far from any lake or pond.

The pilot pushes the throttle to full open position as the tail of the seaplane squats low in the water. With the nose of the seaplane in a nose high attitude the floats begin to plow their way through the water throwing water spray in all directions.

Slowly, the pilot relaxes his pressure on the control and the nose of the seaplane begins to level off. The engine is groaning for all its worth with that big load, trying to get up enough speed to lift off the water in time to clear the mountain.

Luckily, a good headwind helped lift the seaplane to higher altitudes just enough to clear the treetops. The passengers wipe the sweat off their foreheads and sit back with a sigh of relief. They are on their way to their destination, a log cabin on a lake far out in the wilderness and out of contact with civilization.

Maybe, if they are lucky, they might be given the use of a short wave radio to keep in touch with the seaplane base in case someone gets hurt, or lost. Better yet, in case the seaplane doesn't show up for a few days beyond their scheduled pickup date. Quite

THE WOES
OF MOOSE HUNTING

often, this time of year brings a lot of snowstorms preventing the seaplanes from flying. The hunters run low on food, and the first thing you know, "PANIC." "Where's that damn airplane? It's supposed to have been here three days ago."

People that go back in the bush have to realize it's different than being in the city. You just can't have things go like you want all the time. Being back in the bush and out of touch with the normal routine of living brings your life more to reality. You have to make do with what you have and learn to survive under different circumstances.

Having the comforts of a cabin, whether it is made of plywood over a two by three frame, or a log cabin, has its advantages over a tent or piece of plastic thrown over a few poles tied to several trees. At least in the comforts of a nice dry heated cabin the hunter can dry his clothes from a long day out in the bush trudging in heavy wet snow, or from being soaked to the hide from a steady downpour.

Making a camp out of plastic is crude and not always the most comfortable. Three feet of snow can ruin a plastic camp in a hurry. All of those clothes that supposedly were tucked away in a safe place are found completely drenched as the moose hunter drags his weary body back into camp after a long day's hunt.

Not only does he find his clothing soaked, but his eyes fall on his stash of food spread all over the ground buried under the snow. Those nice fresh loaves of bread he just purchased from the store moments before he boarded the aircraft are all soaked and mushy and unfit to eat.

THE WOES
OF MOOSE HUNTING

If you think that's bad, how about crawling into a sleeping bag that is totally drenched. Well, this is called roughing it. Some hunters don't care too much for this sort of thing. I don't know as I blame them for thinking that way. Since I was a kid at the age of eleven, I did what I called roughing it.

At first, when I was young and didn't know any better, I thought I was enjoying that kind of life out in the bush. Now that I am older and nearly seventy years under my belt, I find the comforts of a log cabin more to my liking.

When I look back over the many years that I spent roughing it with a piece of plastic thrown over me, or sleeping in a small tent smelling each others feet, I often ask myself, "who in their right mind would do a thing like that?" There were times when there was no room to roll over without someone yelling, "get over there." The snoring would be so loud, it seemed like a freight train was rumbling down the tracks within a few feet of the tent.

All in all, people that take on the spirit of a moose hunt have to put all these things to the side and say, "Ain't we having fun!"

Keeping the rifles dry and oiled is probably one of the most important responsibilities a hunter has. If his rifle isn't clean, there's going to be trouble. I took a fellow out hunting one day and showed him one of the nicest bucks you would ever want to lay eyes on. Well would you know, his gun misfired. It was a cold day, and this fellow had been hunting for a week in snowy conditions. I asked him, "when was the last time you cleaned that gun of yours?" His answer was, "I haven't shot my gun for quite a while, I didn't think I

THE WOES
OF MOOSE HUNTING

needed to clean it." Now I happen to know that any good hunter takes great pride in his weapons. Maybe I don't have to tell you, but he didn't get his trophy buck that day. I had shown him the same buck several times that particular day and I was wondering how come his gun didn't go off when he kept pulling his gun to his shoulder. Now you know the rest of the story.

Knowing the area that one hunts is a big plus, but what if you have never been back in the bush hundreds of miles from civilization. Much of the territory in Quebec, Canada north of St. Michel Des Saints has low lands and rolling hills with many scattered lakes and beaver dams. It is an ideal habitat for moose. Much of the area has been logged off allowing new tree growth and raspberry bushes to spring up.

Heavy growths of fur trees dominate much of the low lands providing good cover for moose. One of the major problems of hunting in these areas is that it makes it tough for a hunter to find his way around. If he isn't able to read his compass well, he can get lost very easily.

Because there are so many small lakes and ponds throughout the forest a hunter can miss seeing a lake when going into the woods. When he is on his way back out to his camp or point of origin, he may come onto a lake and not understand how come. He becomes confused and starts to wonder if his compass is working okay, or if he got screwed up.

Experienced as I am, I have had to climb a tree to figure out what lake I left my seaplane on. That could be a major catastrophe. It is a big help if hunters take a look around and get familiar with the surrounding

THE WOES
OF MOOSE HUNTING

hills to have an idea which way to go. Of course, that doesn't help if it's storming out and you don't have the visibility. It then becomes a case of being able to read the compass properly. Otherwise, forget it, you are more than likely going to get lost in a big way.

There have been many times in the past where hunters have told me what good woodsmen they are, how they never get lost. My experience when I hear that is to take their statement with a grain of salt. I have spent many hours and days looking for those that have said that very same thing.

Moose hunting can bring a lot of grief for loved ones at home waiting for the return of a family member that rushed off to get his first moose. Maybe the airplane crashed flying the hunter into the bush, or on the way out with his kill. Hopefully, everything went well and the hunter returns home with a big smile and hug.

When a hunter comes face to face with a big old bull moose and he sees the eyes of the moose rolled back in its socket, it's time to get out of its way. During the rutting season a moose is not to be trusted. It can charge a person in an instant. I can't think of anything worse than being charged by a bull moose and have him drive its antlers into your body and carry you off into the woods never to be found. Only a few pieces of clothing might be found leaving a clue to the person who was wearing that particular piece of clothing.

On one of my moose hunts a few years back, I had flown some friends into a remote lake surrounded by swampland and bogs with only a few low lying hills. A heavy growth of fur trees lined the shoreline making it tough to see very far beyond the edges of the lake.

THE WOES
OF MOOSE HUNTING

Determined as usual, I led my friends through the forest to explore what lie beyond. If we could only pick up a fresh moose track we could track it down and hopefully have at least one moose.

Having to push the thick growth of fur branches to the side, we clawed our way through the dense forest. Eventually, we made our way into the depths of a huge swamp with grass up to our thighs. Alder bushes stood tall throughout the swamp and in some places we trudged through water up to the tops of our hip boots. It wasn't exactly what I called easy going. This is what some people call fun just to get a moose.

One of the better parts of the whole thing, is that moose like this kind of environment. They love feeding on alder bushes and the green vegetation in the swamps. It wasn't long before we came across several moose tracks. Sloshing around in all that muck and trying to sort out the moose tracks gave us a little problem, but woe and behold, I spotted a moose cutting down a few alder branches.

People think moose hunting is fairly easy and it's like walking up to a cow in a field and dropping it. Well, I can tell you I have found that to be quite the contrary. I have hunted moose that have been every bit as wild as any white tail deer could ever be, and I have chased them through some of the thickest and smallest openings through trees and thick brush that only a rabbit could squeeze through.

Maybe, there have been a few times when I found it to be extra easy to get a moose, but this wasn't one of those times. I gave my friend the opportunity to shoot his first moose, but in all the anxiety the moose hunt turned into a fiasco.

THE WOES
OF MOOSE HUNTING

I guess my friend got a little nervous and buck fever set in. I could see his rifle barrel going around in circles and hot steam rising out of his mouth. When I looked at his face a little closer, I could see sweat beads dripping from his forehead and the look of anxiety in his eyes. I had seen this many times before and in most cases it could only spell trouble.

Some hunters would be squeezing the trigger with all their might trying to get that first shot off and nothing happens. All the time that huge trophy moose or deer is standing there looking right at him and I'm saying, "shoot, shoot, he's going to take off." When he raises his tail and perks up his ears, he's gone. All you're going to see are his hind feet disappearing in the bush.

When the silence finally broke as a shot rang out, I saw a limping moose disappear out of sight and headed for the hills. The moose had been struck low in the front quarter and I knew from past experience we were in for a long chase.

Because of so many moose tracks in the area, it was difficult to distinguish the difference from the wounded moose when it occasionally stopped bleeding. Much of the tracking involved rushing to the top of a hill to look out across the area to see if we could see the moose.

By now the moose was in high gear and headed for some unknown territory, and as the day wore on I began to have second thoughts about continuing the chase.

Letting a wounded animal go was not one of my beliefs. Our bodies were beginning to show some wear and tear so I figured we had better head back to

THE WOES
OF MOOSE HUNTING

the seaplane. Maybe we could spot the moose from the air and finish it before darkness overtook us.

About ten miles north of where we had first wounded the moose I spotted a moose laying near a small bog with its ears pinned back indicating that it may be wounded. Landing the seaplane within walking distance was the next thing.

Landing on a small lake is not the best of choices, but we were fighting time so in wc wcnt. If worco came to worse, I would have to make several trips out of the small lake to a larger lake and reload all the moose meat to fly it back to camp.

As it was, it was a long trek over the hills to where we could look down upon the same moose we had wounded. By this time, the anxiety had worn off and after a careful and well-aimed shot my friend claimed his moose.

With what little strength we had left we were dragging our feet over the rough terrain, and carrying the moose quarters didn't help. By the time we got the moose meat out to the seaplane it was almost dark making it late getting back to camp. I think this would be a good lesson for those that can't calm themselves down and take the time to make a well placed shot.

The business of chasing a wounded moose or deer for miles and miles through swamp and rugged country is for the birds.

This was just one of many episodes of the woes of moose hunting. We never had the use of a bulldozer or four-wheeler to haul a moose out with. There have been times when a hunter would wound a moose in the bush and have it head for the nearest lake or pond. The moose decides it's going to swim across

THE WOES
OF MOOSE HUNTING

the lake to get away from us and drops dead out in the middle of the lake.

The next scene is the hunter is standing on the shore of the lake scratching his head wondering how he is going to retrieve the moose with no canoe or boat. Maybe the thought of building a raft out of some dead trees, but that's not really a good idea. What if the raft starts to sink and he falls into the freezing water. He may not make it to shore before the cold water gets the best of him and he becomes another statistic.

That's where I come in. So we all jump in the seaplane and taxi out to where the moose is, hook a rope on it and drag it to shore. The job isn't over yet. Try cutting up the moose in the lake. It weighs too much to drag it upon the shore so the struggle of cutting it up in the water is an unbelievable task. Every time this happens, I swear it will be the last.

If only I didn't enjoy being a bush pilot and guide so much, I probably wouldn't have had to deal with so many of these situations. But......, I guess I was born to roam the wilds of the unknown and bring a lot of hair raising adventures to those that dare fly with me.

Being grounded for three days in a snowstorm that dumped three feet of snow on the ground was quite interesting. My seaplane sat on a lake near Chibougamou in northern Quebec in a blinding snowstorm for three days. All of the smaller lakes had frozen over and all we could see was white. Trees were bent over laden with heavy wet snow making it almost impossible to make our way through the forest.

The moose season was coming to a close and with the worst conditions I had seen in years. I was begin-

THE WOES
OF MOOSE HUNTING

ning to wonder if any of us would have a chance to fill our tags. The seaplane was covered with so much snow I didn't think we would ever get it cleaned off enough to fly.

The floats were coated with several inches of ice caused from the freezing water as it splashed over the floats. The only way I could free up the control cables for the rudders on the floats was to first break all the ice from them and then pour crankcase oil on the pulleys to keep them from freezing.

It was a sorry situation to say the least, but you know how it is when you want to go hunting. Sometimes old "Mother Nature" can really show her wrath and there is nothing you can do about it. You grit your teeth and say, "no problem, we can handle it." That attitude can get you into trouble sometimes.

Once we got a slight break in the weather I decided if we were going to get a moose we had better do something about it, snowstorm or no snowstorm. It was almost twelve o'clock noon before we managed to get into the air and fly south to a place that I had seen moose a few days past. If you want an eerie feeling, try flying in a world of frozen wasteland covered with three feet of snow and no life moving about.

With the combination of strong northwest winds and blowing snow squalls and flying at treetop level, it was a rough flight getting to our next destination. The North Country had been dealt a hard blow weatherwise and it looked like winter had set in for good. It was like we were the only ones left in the world flying around the wilds of the north hoping to find a moose or two. This was one of those challenges that met me head on.

THE WOES
OF MOOSE HUNTING

The look of concern, and maybe a little fright show-ed only too clearly on the faces of my friends. I could see their doubts as to whether or not we would be able to get back home, let alone getting any moose. Through a lot of determination and the drive I had within to have a successful hunt, I managed to fly us to a lake with an open area big enough to land on.

I taxied the seaplane close to the mouth of a small stream that emptied into the lake where we all got out with our hip boots on, and in snow up to our waist. This had gone from an enjoyable moose hunt to just plain crazy. Who in their right mind would want to put up with these kind of conditions. It's cheaper to go to the local store and by a beef. But if you did that, there wouldn't be any moose stories to tell your grand chil-dren about.

Moose are known to hang around water, and usual-ly where there is a brook there are alder bushes that the moose like to feed on. The only problem was, the woods were covered with so much snow we couldn't see a snowshoe rabbit if it was sitting five feet in front of us.

We had a tough time wallowing in the deep snow as we made our way single file along the bank of the brook. As we lifted one foot at a time we made our way through the forest. First one person would break trail, and then another. Then the big surprise of our life, three moose lay in a huddle just in front of us. A large bull, a younger bull, and a cow half buried in snow lay quietly not expecting any intrusion into their world that had been surrounded by a vicious storm.

Our moose hunt could be over within minutes if only things could go right for a change. There would

THE WOES
OF MOOSE HUNTING

be a moose for each of us. As we crept slowly towards the three moose we made our plan. On the count of three, we would all take our shots at the moose we had selected. When the shooting was over, the big bull lay wounded with his head held high and the other two had come to their end.

Snow from the nearby trees came tumbling down on his head covering it with a white blanket. I tried to convince one of the fellows to go up to the moose and brush the snow off of his head so I could take his picture, but all I could hear was. "Are you crazy? No way am I going to do that, you want to get me killed."

So as it turned out, the great white hunter, bush pilot and whatever, made his way up to the moose to reach out and gently brushed the snow from his head, then stepped back and took his picture. I guess the moose wasn't feeling the greatest so he didn't offer to give me much of a hassle.

Getting the three moose was one thing, but getting them out to civilization was another. I flew back into Chibougamou to see about hiring a helicopter or maybe hire some Indians to come and help carry out the moose.

I soon came to the conclusion that nobody wanted to do anything in the kind of snow conditions that surrounded us. Usually, I could find a few Indians willing to jump at the opportunity to make a few bucks, but not today. As far as the mining company that owned the helicopters, it was either way too expensive, or that they couldn't fly the moose out for several days. Needless to say, it was very discouraging, but not too unexpected. I think that sometimes the people up in the North Country just don't have the spirit that I do.

THE WOES
OF MOOSE HUNTING

We were now fighting for time. Everything was freezing up. If we didn't get on the ball and get the moose out soon, it would be too late. It was several hours flying time to fly south to St. Michel Des Saints to where we had a vehicle to transport the moose back home to New Hampshire. I would have to make several trips to do all this and between the wicked snow conditions and the weather, it meant I would be one busy bush pilot for a couple of days.

Having the moose meat spoil was the last thing we needed to worry about due to the frigid conditions. I didn't have the most rugged individuals with me at the time, but with a little coaxing and nudging I managed to get them into high gear and haul the moose meat out to the seaplane. I had to tell them. "Look, grit your teeth and tell yourself you have to do it, and that's that."

Being a bush pilot and guide for so many years brings me into contact with so many different kinds of people that I must admit, it does present a challenge at times.

To end this particular story, it was two days before my friends were headed back to New Hampshire with their moose. Weary, cold, tired, and I am sure full to the hilt of moose hunting, especially in the conditions that was brought on us by good old "Mother Nature," they will remember this trip for the rest of their days.

Battling the elements that worsens towards the end of moose season because winter creeps in on you so suddenly, brings a big challenge to any bush pilot or hunter that wants to push things to the extreme. Perhaps it would be better planning a hunt during the first part of the hunting season when the weather is much

THE WOES
OF MOOSE HUNTING

nicer. I have known a few hunters to fall asleep next to a lake while waiting for me to push some moose in their direction.

The rumble of the moose's hooves vibrating the ground they were sleeping on woke them up only in time to see the tails of the moose disappear out of sight. When I got a chance to talk to them, I asked for an explanation as to why they didn't get the moose. "Oh, it was so nice and comfortable in the sun, we just fell asleep. Sorry about that."

At times, I break my back putting in a big effort trying to help these people get their game, I almost wonder if they really appreciate it. The person that gave me the most grief, I have put them in the worst possible places where you least expect an animal to go. So what happens, he turns out to be the one that the animals go to. "Bang, he gets his game." Sometimes I just can't win.

After a long week of trudging through the hills and swamps, and the sweat of lugging out your moose, you would think your hunt was successful. That is not always true. I had set up a camp for some friends for moose hunting, but what was to happen later in the week was a struggle for survival and trying to save several moose quarters hanging on a pole.

Here again, it was late in the season. The forest was covered with snow letting us know that winter was here. It seems that once the ground is covered with snow, the animals in the woods find it more difficult to find food. In the case of wolves, it is no different. I had seen several wolves in the area while hunting moose, but as a rule we don't worry about them.

They generally slink through the forest unnoticed,

THE WOES
OF MOOSE HUNTING

keeping themselves in low areas or behind a thicket hiding them from view. One time, while watching a huge white wolf making his way through the woods, I thought about shooting it. I held my rifle ready, aiming it at a clearing thinking the wolf would appear.

As it turned out, the wolf made a detour through a hollow behind some brush avoiding the clearing. I got a glimpse of him once and a while but never had a chance to shoot it. It's like they have a sixth sense about something not being quite right to avoid trouble.

The wolves occasionally manage to pull down a moose or two to have a nice delicious steak, but for some reason or other they decided to sneak into our camp and steal our moose quarters hanging on a pole that was stretched between two trees.

At first, they were quiet while they were at their little tricks, but I guess they got to arguing over who was going to have what and started kicking up a ruckus.

It woke up everyone in the tent and all heck broke loose. The wolves were stubborn as all get out and thought they wanted the moose meat more than they wanted their lives.

By the time the shooting was over three wolves had been killed and the others scattered for their lives.

Most of the moose meat had been ripped to shreds leaving us no choice but to hunt for another moose. My fellow hunters had never experienced this sort of adventure, and from then on there wasn't much sleep.

I always figured it must have been a band of outlaw wolves roaming the forest for whatever they could sink their teeth into, even if they had to rob a poor hunter's catch. People that go on a moose hunt are not aware of all of these strange happenings.

THE WOES
OF MOOSE HUNTING

After all the preparation of buying new equipment and clothing for that long awaited moose hunt, there is nothing worse than to be flown into an area that has no moose.

Some hunters that I have known have not dared venture too far back in the bush to seek out a moose. Whether it was a case of being afraid of getting lost, or perhaps it was a case where they may have expected a moose to come into their camp to be shot, I don't really know.

It is no small fee when a person adds up all of his expenses to go on a hunt. One of the bigger expenses is the cost of getting flown in to where you want to hunt. The cost of getting to the seaplane base from home, the food, all the hunting gear, and maybe you have to purchase a new rifle because your old one isn't good enough. When all these expenses are totaled up, your wife asks, "don't you think you have spent enough for one week of fun?"

Nothing aggravates a man any more than a wife questioning the reasons why a man does what he does, or what he needs for his hunting or fishing trip. After all, isn't he an adult and old enough to decide for himself.

No matter what the decision, when a group of hunters are flown in to a remote lake and gets dropped off for a week or two with promises there are plenty of moose in the area, they are usually stuck there until the seaplane comes in to pick them up.

Maybe the sky was overcast when the seaplane disappears over the horizon after leaving you standing at the shoreline of the lake next to a makeshift camp. Then the sky starts to thicken with heavy wet

THE WOES
OF MOOSE HUNTING

snowflakes. The dread of being snowed in for the week starts to sink in. All of a sudden you feel abandoned, alone in a strange wilderness. You start to panic, and you ask yourself, can you handle this? Is there going to be any moose around to shoot? How about the other guys, are they going to get along with me? Is everyone going to do his share of things to make it a happy week?

One thing for sure, you are not going to hike it back in to civilization. You have to make the best of what you have so you may as well make up your mind to it. When winter sets in and the snow starts piling up, the moose head for the hills to yard up for the winter. There is one problem. Trying to find where the moose have yarded up is the big question.

Having your own airplane is a big help. You can have the benefit of flying over the area you want to hunt to see what it looks like, or maybe if you are lucky, when the airplane you were flown in by, circled the area you were going to camp, you may have seen some moose sign. Usually, the bush pilot will oblige you if you ask him to fly you around the area before dropping you off.

If a hunter isn't very sure of himself in the woods, he can mark a line through the woods with plastic tape to let him know how to get back out to camp. That is, if he follows the tape in the right direction. It is always a good idea to check your compass every few minutes to give you an idea which direction you are hunting in. This allows you to pick a more direct route back to where you first started.

Becoming familiar with your compass before starting out on a hunt is always the best way to go. I don't

THE WOES
OF MOOSE HUNTING

know how many times I have flown people back in the bush professing to be great outdoorsmen and the first thing I find out, someone got lost. It is time consuming and frustrating spending hours and days looking for these people.

Because of so many lakes in the North Country, it is very easy to get confused. I have flown moose hunters into areas where there was a dozen moose. When the hunters went off into the bush they found it difficult to keep track of which lake they were on. They got so involved chasing moose they lost all senses of their whereabouts. When they didn't show up back at camp come nightfall, I got very concerned.

As the hours ticked by and no signs of the missing hunter, all sorts of things came to my mind. Thoughts of whether the person had a heart attack being so on edge about finding his way back to camp, or if he followed the moose way out of the area and not realizing it, were two possibilities. But what if he was just plain lost and wandering through the night blind and no idea where he was.

It is a big responsibility on my part to make sure the people I fly back in the bush get back home in one piece safe and sound. On the crack of dawn, I am up in the air searching every bog, hilltop or high point looking for the first sign of life. Maybe, if I am lucky, I might see a puff of smoke rising from a wooded area signaling for help. Some of the hunters have strayed so far out of the area it was a day and a half before I was able to locate them with the airplane.

Thank heaven in all the years that I have flown people north caribou hunting and moose hunting, I haven't lost anyone yet. Fortunately, they had a bush

THE WOES
OF MOOSE HUNTING

pilot that understood the wilds of the north and had the sixth sense to find them. I have had people just give up with the idea they were going to freeze to death and that nobody was going to save them.

I know from experience, that if I hadn't had the airplane to search for these people, they definitely would have perished. I would not have been able to cover the vast amount of territory necessary in time to save them. The elements of the weather would claim their lives in a matter of a few short days at the most.

When outfitters fly hunters back in the bush to be dropped off to hunt on their own, the hunters are left totally at the mercy of whatever happens during that week. A hunter may cut himself with a chainsaw or axe so seriously that he needs the attention of a doctor, or he may bleed to death before he gets flown to a hospital.

There are so many things that can happen on a moose hunt that can create so much havoc I try to screen the people I fly to help eliminate the possibility of trouble. Thus the woes of moose hunting will continue as long as people will venture forth into the wilds for their quest for a moose or two.

THE LIFE
OF A BUSH PILOT

Depending on whether it's a sporting camp, an outfitter, or a seaplane base that employs a bush pilot, it may make all the difference in the world the type of flying a bush pilot does. He may even fly for a fishery along the Alaska coastline. Each type of flying has its own, let's say "calling."

No matter what the type of flying, there is always a certain amount of risk involved. A pilot has to take everything into consideration, but most certainly doesn't look for things to happen. I am sure he does his best under any circumstances, but there are times when his luck just runs out. It then becomes a case of survival. How he handles the situation he is confronted with makes the difference between life and death.

The bush pilot that works for a seaplane base is perhaps more fortunate. For the most part, his daily flying represents flying people within a few miles of the seaplane base to a camp on a lake with plenty of room for taking off and landing. He isn't generally subject to having to land in small beaver dams or rivers that he has to dodge rocks or stumps.

As a rule, he is able to come back to a nice warm comfortable bed and a hot meal cooked by his wife or girl fiend. Either that or he enjoys a nice meal prepared by the chef at the restaurant at the seaplane base. As a rule, he is not subject to long hauls for hundreds of miles where he can encounter several

THE LIFE
OF A BUSH PILOT

different weather patterns. Perhaps he may get forced down on some remote lake by a fierce snowstorm and have to rough it for a few days.

He has to get out the tent or make a makeshift camp out of plastic and try his level best to keep his passengers calmed down. After all, they only have a week to go fishing or hunting, and they don't want to waste it hanging around stuck in the bush unable to do their thing.

The seaplane base has its exceptions as far as the bush pilot is concerned. When it comes time for the caribou season to roll around seaplane bases from all over the Province of Quebec are engaged in the job of flying hunters to the far north. This entails many long and arduous flights to outfitter's camps scattered across northern Quebec and Labrador. Seaplanes of all kinds as well as airplanes on wheels crisscross the North Country.

Someone would think there was a gold rush going on in the North Country with all the activity. But instead, this is called the hunting fever. Bush pilots are kept busy from dawn until dark flying people back into the bush. Come snow, rain, or fog, the bush pilot is churning his way through all kinds of weather. It is a good thing his passengers don't really know some of the dangers involved in flying in these kind of conditions. They figure the pilot is in control and should know what he is doing. "I hope he does."

About the only thing that stops a bush pilot from flying, is if the wind is too severe, or the visibility is down to ground zero. That's when he can't see the nose of the airplane or the treetops under him. Playing tag with the treetops isn't much fun, especially

THE LIFE
OF A BUSH PILOT

when you have passengers on board. Maybe one of the trees sticking up is a little taller than others, and "whacko," either the floats of the airplane takes a head on hit, or the propeller starts chewing up some bark. If the treetop isn't too thick through, you might make it to the next one. Otherwise, you could be sitting amongst a pile of scrapped aluminum wondering what happened.

I have known certain bush pilots brag how they clipped a few treetops, either on takeoff, or flying too low. I have been guilty of picking up a few lily pads with my floats when lifting off at the very last moment at the end of a small lake or pond. A bush pilot has to know his aircraft pretty well when he does these sorts of things, but let's not make a habit of it. It makes the passengers a little nervous if you know what I mean.

Though there is a gross weight limit for each aircraft, the people that the bush pilot flies don't seem to take that into consideration. They bring everything they can squeeze into their vehicle and expect the pilot to just pile it in the airplane. In some cases, they plead innocent. They didn't know the aircraft had a limit on how much it can carry. "Well, we will leave so and so at the seaplane base, maybe if you are coming this way, you can bring him in later. We have to get our gear into camp first."

Bush flying can be a joke at times, but for the most part, it is serious business, and the quicker a pilot knows this, the better off he will be. There are times when the bush pilot has to be strict with his passengers. If he lets his passengers call the shots or makes a decision for him, he could be in deep trouble. He has to be the one in command and the only one to

THE LIFE
OF A BUSH PILOT

make the decisions. Otherwise, I don't' think I would be flying with him.

There have been many times when my passengers would try to put pressure on me to fly in bad weather when I didn't think it was safe to fly. I would say, "look if you want to live to fish another day, leave the decisions up to me."

I think I would rather put my trust in a pilot that has been flying in the North Country for quite a few years with a lot of experience under his belt than listen to someone who has no idea about flying.

The bush pilot that flies for a fishing lodge in Alaska has a relatively easy job. His job is to fly clients to local rivers and lakes for the day and perhaps acts as a guide as well. At lunchtime, he may help cook a fresh caught salmon with a little touch of lemon, butter and salt and pepper over an open fire. After his day out with the sportsmen, he is back at the lodge in time for a well-prepared supper.

If the lodge happens to take in hunters, that's a different story. Then it is up to the bush pilot to fly their clients to arranged places for bear hunting or caribou hunting. It may also be the job of the bush pilot to set up out-camps for moose hunters. The bush pilot may have a variety of duties having to do with the different seasons involved. He is a man of many professions.

Most of my flying career as a bush pilot I have been a one-man operation. Just my Cessna 206 and me. I have had as many as thirty-five moose hunters camped out on nine different lakes over the course of one week and if you don't think I was some busy, think again.

Flying from one camp to the other, checking on the

THE LIFE
OF A BUSH PILOT

hunters to see if they were all okay was a big job in itself. When someone got lost for a few days, or had an accident, I would have to spend many long hours searching for them, or flying a person into civilization to a hospital.

Fuel for the airplane was at a premium, and if I didn't watch my fuel closely, I would end up flying on fumes to get me back to a seaplane base to where I could refuel. Though I always carried extra fuel in plastic fuel cans, it never seemed to be enough to get me by.

Running my fuel tanks in the airplane completely dry isn't a good idea. When the fuel gauges read a little towards the empty mark I would tip the wings from left to right to see which tank had the most fuel. I would then keep switching the fuel valve from the left tank to the right tank with the idea I could keep a little fuel for reserve just in case it came in handy.

The old rule of keeping forty-five minutes fuel reserve doesn't apply much in the North Country, but if only I could have adhered to that rule it would have saved a few passengers from fright. The lower the fuel gauges read, the whiter the passengers got. I would say, "what's the matter boys, don't you like living on the edge?" I used to chuckle when I got into tight spots. It kind of made my day. Anything to throw a little fun into the show, I say.

I never could understand some of my passengers. They either couldn't take a joke, or they didn't care too much for what I called fun. Sticking your neck out shooting the rapids with a Cessna 206 raised a few eyebrows. My friends used to say, "Richard, we have never seen this done before." On some occasions, I might agree with them. I would say to them, "you probably won't see this done again, either."

Without the bush pilot making his work a little fun, it could be boring, but somehow that may pose a question or two. During mid summer, depending on where the bush pilot is working, the flying can slow down leaving the bush pilot to lay around the seaplane base wondering when his next customer will show up. He may get out the cards and play some cribbage or if no one else is around he may be forced to play solitaire.

If he gets bored too much, he may just tell the owner of the seaplane base, "look, I am going down the road for awhile, I'll be back." I never had that problem working for myself. I always had plenty to do flying back to back trips all season long. Some of my flying kept me in the air for twelve hours or so on different days. When I stepped out of the seaplane I felt like I was walking on a cloud.

Being a guide as well as a bush pilot, and owning my own business, it was up to me to do my own bookings, making personal contacts to solicit business, service my own seaplane, and do all the planning of trips. My life as a bush pilot has been so much different than other bush pilots working for someone else. I had the freedom to do what I wanted to do and run the show as I saw fit.

Some pilots may think that flying is flying, but only after a bush pilot has gone on his own to feel the freedom of flying where he chooses can he realize the big difference between working for himself or working for someone else. Of course, he has to have his own airplane, and that costs some bucks. The high cost of insuring the airplane for liability and hull damage would give some would-be airplane owners the shivers. Then you have the maintenance and the inspections to deal with. Annual inspections these days cost big money. After all that, you have to overhaul the propeller after a certain amount of hours. That's more big bucks.

Depending on how many hours a pilot flies his airplane in a given year, he can estimate his hourly cost to fly. The individual expenses can be tallied up and divided by the hours he flies to give him an idea how much in dollars he has to get per hour to operate.

The one major cost that can sneak up on the owner of an aircraft is the cost to overhaul the engine. This also has to be figured in when adding up the costs of flying. When a pilot stops to think about all these expenses and reaches into his pocket to see how much money he has, he perhaps will think twice about owning his own airplane.

I just thought I would throw in this bit of information in case you just bought your first airplane without stopping to realize how much it costs to fly. A lot of pilots find out the hard way and find themselves forced to sell their airplane because they don't have the extra cash to maintain and operate the airplane once they have purchased it.

I know of one person that bought a new Cessna 206 and had planned to put it on floats. When he found out how much the floats costs, he put the aircraft up for sale. I'll bet you can't guess who bought it? I enjoyed flying this aircraft for many years, especially after I got a set of floats installed.

Speaking of floats, choosing the right float for your particular use is very important. Some floats have a much flatter bottom on them, making it rough landing in choppy water. Over time, it can raise havoc with your seaplane pounding it to bits.

The continued rough landings can put extra fatigue on the aluminum and framework of the aircraft, loosening rivets and all sorts of things. It can pound the dash so badly, it can cause you extra problems with the radio equipment, loosen windshields and end up losing the value of the aircraft.

It is good to check the fuselage for loose rivets. You can tell when they have worked loose by inspecting each rivet to see if there is any dirt or grey around the head of the rivet.

Continued landing in rough water will eventually loosen rivets. Then the airplane will start racking and act like it is falling apart. Of course, this is speaking to the extreme, but it does happen.

This is where the "v brace" a v shaped tubing at the inside of the windshield comes in handy. It helps reinforce the dash and windshield frame of the cockpit to keep the windshield from popping out on a real rough landing or takeoff.

There are several manufacturers of floats and it is up to the individual to decide which float he prefers. I chose the "PK" floats because the bottoms have a steeper angle to them allowing me to handle more rough water. Other float designs may or may not get you off the water as quick, but for the sake of not beating my seaplane to death flying for so many years in extremely rough water, I prefer the "PKs."

A pilot may not have the choice of where he lands when he arrives at his destination. If the wind gets so strong that the waves become so huge, you may have

THE LIFE
OF A BUSH PILOT

no choice but to land. You may not have the extra fuel on board to fly out of that kind of condition. Of course, if you are lucky, you might find a quiet cove to land in.

When flying long distance, you stand a very good chance of running into a few weather changes making it impossible to predict what kind of conditions you will wind up flying in.

On one occasion, I had flown seven and a half hours through beautiful weather, but when I arrived at my camp the wind was blowing like seventy miles an hour. I knew if I landed out in the lake, the waves were so huge they would have knocked the floats out from under us. It would have been suicide. I told the friends of mine to hang on and cinch up their seat belt a notch or two, that I was going to slow fly the seaplane right up to the beach that was protected by an esker.

Because the wind speed was much faster than the stall speed of the Cessna, I was able to drop my flaps to twenty degrees, back off on the throttle and practically hover over the beach at stall speed and set it down. This surprised my friends a bit. They remarked, "We have done a lot of bush flying before, but have never seen anything like this." I told them, "you will probably not see this done again, that I am all done flying in such bad conditions." That is, for now.

I guess that is the reason why I chose the profession of a bush pilot. There was always a new challenge to keep me on the edge. How dull my life would have been if I hadn't gotten into flying, dealing with what "Mother Nature" dishes out to me. I keep telling her to give me a break and go and pick on someone else for a change, give me a break. That went over like a lead balloon.

The life of a bush pilot brings a lot of adventure. No two trips are ever the same. I find that getting to meet so many different kinds of people is quite interesting. Some are so serious when they go on a trip, and others seem to be in a joking mood and always in high spirits.

Some clients put on the act of knowing all there is to know about hunting and life in the bush when in reality, they don't understand much at all. As soon as I spend a little time with them, I read them like a book.

My biggest concern flying people back in the bush is to try my best to give them a good and successful trip, and to make their trip an enjoyable one. Above all, I stress the importance of doing things in a lawful way. The last thing I want to happen is to have my aircraft seized because of some illegal act. I have to play the part of a game warden most of the time to keep everyone out trouble.

People think, that because they are hundreds of miles from civilization, they are free to do what they want. I have been surprised more than once by a Mounted Policeman or game warden.

Off in the distance I would hear an airplane approaching while I have been fishing or hunting on a remote river or lake. Then the sound of the engine slowing down as the airplane circles overhead. The next moment, a DeHavilland Beaver is pulling up next to my seaplane and the long arm of the Law steps out to check us out.

I value my airplane more than wanting to take a chance to have my airplane seized. Even a small

THE LIFE
OF A BUSH PILOT

thing like forgetting to unload a rifle is cause to have the airplane seized. It's worse when a client tells the game warden as the airplane is being searched not to touch his rifle it's loaded.

Not only is the job of the bush pilot to fly the airplane, but a lot of times, his job is to do the cooking, dressing off the game or fish, guiding the clients he flies, as well as watching over them. He has to find a smooth area to set the tent on in case they have to pitch the tent. He can't have roots of trees or rocks sticking up into someone's rib cage or backbone while they are trying to get some sleep.

Being a first time experience for some of the people I have flown, it becomes a learning experience for them. Most of them are able to handle things well and adapt to the living in the wilds like a professional. I do my best to work with my clients in every way possible to bring pleasure to their trip.

It would be impossible to think that everyone has the capabilities to know how to get along in the wilderness with the bare necessities, but I am sure when they arrive back home after their hunting or fishing trip is over, they will have a few stories to tell.

A bush pilot never knows for sure what kind of mechanical problems he is apt to run into while flying in the North Country. He may accidentally damage a float on landing by striking a rock and have to improvise in making a repair in order to get him back into civilization.

Engine problems of one kind or another may occur of which I have been fortunate enough to be able to repair most minor problems with the tools I always carry in the airplane. Thank heaven I have not had an

THE LIFE
OF A BUSH PILOT

engine failure in the North Country in all the years I have flown. That doesn't say I haven't had my share of problems caused by other mechanics when they worked on my airplane near my home.

One mechanic caused me to loose all the engine oil on takeoff when the oil filter adapter blew out of the back end of the engine. If I hadn't have had enough altitude when I got between two hills, I would not have been able to shut the engine down and do a dead-stick landing on a river.

The engine seized solid upon landing bringing a few hectic moments. While the current was taking the seaplane down the river, I had to jump onto the floats with my canoe paddle and paddle for all my life to get the seaplane to shore.

I managed to get a farmer to come to the edge of the river with his bucket loader and lift the engine out so I could rebuild the engine by using parts from an-other spare engine I had purchased from a friend of mine. Three days later, I was on my way to Hudson Bay.

Another time, I had a mechanic overhaul my engine and needless to say, he did a lousy job of it. He didn't give enough clearance on the wrist pins and put the fuel pump gear on backwards which let about one eighth of the gear ride on the other gear. Moments before taking off from a dolly at the airport I was doing a run-up on the engine checking it out, and all of a sudden the engine seizes solid.

The fuel pump gear jumped off the shaft and chew-ed part of the aluminum crankcase putting aluminum shavings all through the engine. The piston pins had seized tight locking up the connecting rods, stopping

THE LIFE
OF A BUSH PILOT

the engine in a hurry. The mechanic had refused to come to the airport to take a look at the engine and I was told I had to bring the engine back to him so he could fix it right. I lost some valuable time as I was supposed to be flying north the next day. That trip got delayed for a few days. I don't have to tell you, there was a big to do about that mess up.

On a real hot day, with temperatures in the nineties I had the seaplane loaded with all the fishing gear and friends ready to fly north. Of all the crazy things to happen. The transfer collar that attaches to the crankshaft decided it was time to be replaced.

The babbit bearing surface had warn to the point when the engine oil got hotter than normal because of a long takeoff and the outside temperature being so warm the oil spilled by the transfer collar back into the oil pan instead of being transferred to the governor.

The governor controls the oil pressure to the variable pitch propeller, which in turn controls the revolutions of the engine. If there isn't enough oil pressure to change the pitch of the propeller to the proper pitch, the engine will race at too high of an "rpm" and could cause the engine to burn up.

The lake I had taken off from was at an altitude of eleven hundred feet. It was a good thing, because I had to back off on the throttle and drop several hundred feet down over a mountain to land on a lake five miles south.

Here again, it was a good thing I knew how to take care of my airplane engine. I had to pull the engine out and take the engine apart to install a new transfer collar. A couple of days later I was on my way to northern Canada.

THE LIFE
OF A BUSH PILOT

I figure the man upstairs was watching over me in all my flying with all the things that has happened. He certainly was watching over me when I had an encounter with a downdraft situation. Luckily, everyone got out of that one safely.

The longer one flies, especially the kind of flying I have done, the better the chances of the "law of averages" will catch up to you. Somewhere, somehow, there will be something out of the ordinary that will sneak up on you and bring you close to the edge of disaster. All the expertise in the world cannot stop things from happening when the ingredients are just right.

It was at the end of moose season in the province of Quebec. My friends had loaded their moose into their vehicle north of Montreal to drive home.

Not knowing what the weather was south into New Hampshire and my wanting to be on the safe side, I called the airport in Montreal for weather. I was told it was beautiful with the winds at about fifteen miles an hour.

My 206 Cessna was running light in weight, for all I had in the airplane was my rifle, sleeping bag, axe, tent, and camera, and about enough fuel to get me home to New Hampshire with a little to spare. Otherwise, I was the sole person in the seaplane.

As I was flying south through the mountains, I encountered several snow squalls, but was able to fly through the low country over the highway.

About the time I arrived at Gaines Mariner at Rouses Point on Lake Champlain to clear the U.S. Customs, the wind was strong out of the south and blowing about seventy miles an hour.

THE LIFE
OF A BUSH PILOT

I could see the huge whitecaps racing down the lake pounding the shoreline and the thoughts of how often the flight service had given me wrong information about the weather.

With no other place to land, and knowing I had to clear customs, I decided to land the seaplane as close to the mariner as possible and take advantage of the breaker wall to get out of the rough water as much as I could. I landed as slowly as I could, skipping from one top of wave to another before finally coming to a stop.

The next thing was to taxi through the rough waves to the dock at Gaines Mariner. It was tough going and after a struggle I managed to secure the seaplane at the dock.

After clearing customs, the customs agent advised me to stay put, that the lake is way too rough to be flying off. He was saying that the excursion boat was not sailing because the powerful winds would blow out its windows and it just wasn't safe. Well, if you knew me, I had flown in some powerful weather and winds plenty of times in the past and figured I could take off in a hurry with such strong winds.

Five minutes later, I am sitting out in front of the dock with the nose of the seaplane headed directly into the wind with my hand on the throttle ready to shove it in for takeoff. A few seconds later, a wicked hurricane force wind coming from my right lifted my right wing into the air tempting to blow the seaplane over onto its back.

I looked over at my left wing to see the wing tip in the water and figured I had better do something in a hurry. It was like I was sitting in a boat with the motor at an idle and all of a sudden a huge wave comes and tips you over. I shoved forward on the throttle, hoping to right the seaplane with the power of the engine, as well as using the controls for the ailerons. It was all to no avail. The wind was so strong the seaplane flipped like it was a turtle being flipped over onto its back.

The seaplane hit the water with such force, the windshield broke on impact and water started rushing in. I said, "Richard, you had better get yourself out of this seaplane in a hurry, or else." Hanging upside down by my seatbelt wasn't my idea of having fun, especially when Lake Champlain was rushing in on me.

After managing to get the cockpit door open, I climbed on top of the floats and hung on for dear life. From the shore, I noticed a small boat with two people in it trying to make their way towards me, but they nearly got swamped. I thought for a moment that they were going to get drowned. While they worked frantically trying to save my seaplane and me from further disaster, the owner of Gaines Mariner came out with his big boat to help out.

For a few minutes it was touch and go as to what may happen, but in the end we managed to drag the seaplane on its back over to calmer waters by the dock. The major problem was unnoticed at the time. My seaplane was dragged across a pile of rocks just under the surface of the water, tearing off the top part of the tail section and damaging the tops of the wings.

The next day, I hired a crane from Platsburgh, N.Y. to lift the seaplane out of the lake, get it right side up and towed it over to the town boat ramp and loaded it onto a flatbed trailer to take home and spend all that

THE LIFE
OF A BUSH PILOT

winter rebuilding it. The next spring I was back to flying up north enjoying some good fishing.

I often wonder to what extent the man upstairs wants to test me. Maybe, he just wants to make sure I have what it takes to be a good bush pilot. I guess I forgot to tell him, I am not out to prove anything, I just want to enjoy my life as a bush pilot.

At present, I unfortunately am without a seaplane, and I don't have to tell you how much I miss the flying. Almost every night I dream of flying a 206 Cessna on floats in one part of the world or the other.

Recently, I had a dream I was flying around the Alps in Europe in wicked bad weather. Rain and fog shrouded the mountains making it almost impossible to fly through. The lack of lakes to land on was putting the pressure on, so to speak, and you know how dreams are at times.

I know I have done the craziest things with my seaplane before, but this one takes the cake. I was forced to land up in the mountains and the only safe place was a huge cave in the side of a mountain. Of course I didn't have any wheels on my floats, but managed to skid the plane inside the cave without any problem.

No sooner had I come to a halt, than an armed guard rushed up to me with an automatic weapon. He told me, "this is restricted territory, it's a gold mine and nobody is allowed in here." For a minute, I thought the guy was going to shoot me. Lucky for me, I woke up from the dream before I figured out how I was going to get out of the cave with the seaplane. Crazy, or what?

Occasionally, for some reason or other, more than likely because of bad weather, I have dreams where

THE LIFE
OF A BUSH PILOT

I landed my seaplane in one of those little watering holes out in a field on a farm. I'm standing beside the seaplane scratching my head wondering how in the world I am going to fly the seaplane out of that fifty-foot pond.

How I got out of that short pond, I couldn't tell you. The next scene was when I was flying up main street in the town next to the farm and trying as hard as I could to miss the electric wires and to find an opening in the trees lined along the street to get up into the open sky. Somehow, I got out of that predicament by waking up. Maybe it was a good thing I woke up before I crashed.

Dreams do some funny things sometimes. I actually have dreamt of things that really happened in real life the following day, or a short time later. I am also glad that some of those dreams didn't really happen in real life. A dream that didn't turn out was a dream I had a couple of nights ago. I dreamt I had bought a new 206 Cessna and it was sitting right next to my bed. Well, dream again Richard, when I finally woke up, what a disappointment, no 206 Cessna.

To get back to the "Life of a bush pilot," what more could a person do to have more of a challenge in his life than to be a bush pilot and have so much fun? It is nice to have people come up to me and say, "remember me? You gave me a seaplane ride, or you took me fishing years ago." They don't like mentioning the times that I saved them from certain death when they got lost for a few days.

Over the years, many would-be pilots have asked the question, "Do you think there will still be a job for a bush pilot in ten or fifteen years? It seems, since the

THE LIFE
OF A BUSH PILOT

airplane was invented, pilots took on the job as bush pilots in one part of the world or the other. We hear about the pilots that flew mail routes through all kinds of weather risking their neck just to get someone's letter to a loved one, or maybe a package that contained medicine to save a person's life.

Yes, even today, the profession of a bush pilot is very important. There are all kinds of needs for a bush pilot, and will be for years to come. Jobs of flying fishermen to flying hunters for caribou, moose and other wild game throughout the world are in demand.

Countries like Africa and Australia offer many interesting challenges for the bush pilot, both on wheels and floats. There is plenty of back-country flying to be done, but I don't know as I care to land in a river full of alligators and have the front of my floats bitten off.

I think I would rather stick to flying in Alaska and northern Canada where I don't have to worry about coming back to my seaplane and find a twenty-foot snake sunning itself on the deck of my floats. I don't know which would be worse to deal with, a grizzly, or the snake.

In my opinion, Alaska has the most to offer for a bush pilot. It certainly is a much bigger challenge as far as flying over and through some of the most rugged mountains a pilot would want to encounter. If a bush pilot is looking for adventure and thrills, Alaska can give him all that he is looking for, and more.

Some of the major problems flying in Alaska are having to deal with the weather while trying to sneak through the mountain passes to get somewhere. There is nothing worse than getting stuck half way though a mountain pass and the weather closes in

THE LIFE
OF A BUSH PILOT

around you blocking your escape. It leaves you no where to go but into the side of a mountain. If the pilot decides to climb up through all the bad weather to get on top of the clouds, he is not guaranteed he will find his way to safety. While he is flying blindly through the storm, he may just wind up crashing into a mountainside.

Too many pilots get killed because they take too many chances. There is a limit to what a pilot calls safe flying, if only he realizes it in time and keeps a cool head.

There are thousands of glaciers all through the mountains in Alaska. Airplanes have been known to crash in them and disappear totally when the airplane eventually gets covered with ice.

Any pilot seeking the life of a bush pilot will find Alaska one of the greatest frontiers to fly in. The great abundance of wildlife, which include deer, moose, caribou, muskox, black bear, grizzlies, wolves, plus many other species of wildlife that would satisfy a sportsman beyond his dreams.

As far as fishing goes, just ask any fisherman that has gone to Alaska to catch the great king salmon, halibut, rainbow trout up to twenty odd pounds, and the sockeye salmon. The many rivers that flow into Cook Inlet from Anchorage to the Bering Sea provide excellent fishing.

Not only is Alaska known for its hunting and fishing, the scenery is just unbelievable with all the glaciers and beautiful lakes. It is a bush pilot's dream to live his life in Alaska doing what he loves best. I will say, that I witnessed some beautiful scenery when I flew around the Yukon and British Columbia.

THE LIFE
OF A BUSH PILOT

Flying as I did throughout the years has brought me some of the fondest memories that a person or pilot could ever expect. I have enjoyed flying in northern Quebec, Canada in the Hudson Bay area and parts of Labrador for many years as a bush pilot, I often say, "I wish I had a dollar for every mile that I have flown in the bush."

Life would be pretty boring without the seaplane, or an airplane on wheels as far as that goes. People that want to get places in a hurry feel that flying is the quickest way to get there, but that isn't always true. How many times has a person been stranded because of bad weather or a breakdown of an airplane.

People that only have a week's vacation can be devastated when their transportation can't make the trip. I've seen sportsmen tearing their hair out, yelling at the owner of the seaplane base, "why can't you fly us in? I have actually witnessed one case where the owner of the seaplane base got so fed up listening to one guy, he decked him and threw him out the door.

In most cases, people just don't have any idea what the weather conditions are like when it comes to flying, and just insist they be flown in to their pre-arranged place. There is nothing worse than to have a bunch of hunters traipsing back and forth in the office building of the seaplane base squawking about the weather and getting everyone disgruntled over things unnecessarily.

The pilots are frustrated enough as it is, and listening to the guys whooping and hollering just makes things worse. I have heard the pilots muttering under their breath, "what's the matter with these jerks, don't

183

they know anything? I don't care if we never fly them. It would be good riddance to them."

I understand the frustration of the hunters or fishermen to a point, but when old "Mother Nature" does her thing, nobody can change it, except her. You have to sit it out and wait for a better day.

I remember a time when I was returning from a caribou trip with some friends from northern Quebec. The weather had turned bad like you would never believe. One right after the other, snowstorms kept us grounded for days.

For four days and four nights I slept out in the open with just a piece of plastic over my sleeping bag and me. Each morning I woke up I had a foot of snow over me, and if you think that wasn't a miserable four days, guess again. My friends were complaining so much, I don't think they would ever go caribou hunting again.

Those are the chances a person takes when flying north. If we could control the weather we would be in our glory.

Thank heaven, not all trips are like that one. I have flown on trips up north when it was like the middle of summer. Not a breeze was stirring and hardly a cloud in the sky. A whole week of that kind of weather could spoil a person real quick, but don't think for one minute you will get a second week of good weather like that. The nice calm sunny days can only mean one thing, a storm is brewing, just give it time.

A STORM'S
FURY UNLEASHES

On a beautiful summer's day in August, the call of the north was sounding out. My son Richard and two of his friends had called me to ask if I would take them to northern Canada fishing. I had only been home for two days from a previous trip and already I was getting bored.

The timing couldn't have been better as the season in the far north was at its peak for when the big trophy speckled brook trout would be in the rivers spawning. I could just picture them in my mind jumping out of the water with a fly hanging tight in their jaw.

During the spawning season the male brook trout take on some of the prettiest colors with their bright red bellies and blue and red spots. Even some of the old male brook trout develop a hooked jaw during the spawning period.

To me, there is nothing like catching one of these trout in the eight to nine pound range. They have that very distinct heavy double tug that tells me I have a big one on and that it is a trout for sure.

With that thought in mind, it didn't take long for me to agree to take my friends on a fishing trip they will never forget. Wasting no time in getting to the dock on Lake Sunapee where I had my 206 Cessna parked, we loaded all the supplies and fishing gear into the seaplane. I had already fueled the airplane to the very top of the wing tanks and loaded some extra fuel cans inside the airplane to get us out of a pinch.

To make sure we have the necessary survival gear on board, I carefully scrutinize everyone's luggage, which would include tents, sleeping bags, one axe, our fishing gear, and plenty of food for the week. No way do I take anyone anywhere unless we have these very important items aboard the airplane. It is has been a firm rule of mine since I first started flying as a bush pilot.

I forgot to mention that my wife wanted to come along as well. There was one condition, having such a big load, that I can manage to get the seaplane off the lake. With calm winds and glassy water, I knew there was going to be trouble lifting off.

The floats were riding low in the water and there was such a heavy feeling on the controls, I figured the airplane was going to struggle on this one. If only there was a little breeze it would help increase the chances for takeoff.

Using up ten miles of lake to try and get in the air made me look a little foolish. Boats kept going by us wondering what in the world am I doing. It was kind of embarrassing in a way, but who could have known how much of a load I was carrying in the seaplane. Only another seaplane pilot may have guessed what the problem was.

With the temperature in the nineties, and the fact of no wind, I had to call on every bit of experience I had to get the right feeling of the seaplane to know when I could get it to lift off the surface of the lake. The lake was at eleven hundred feet in altitude where the air is much thinner making it more difficult to take

A STORM'S
FURY UNLEASHES

off. It would have been much easier if the lake had been at sea level where the air is a lot heavier allowing the propeller to grab more air.

After several attempts to lift off the water, I finally had to flag down some people in a boat passing by to ask if they would be kind enough to take a few of the fuel cans I had on board back to my brother's dock. I hated to disappoint my wife and tell her I couldn't take her with us, so it was a case of sacrificing carrying the extra gas for her.

Soon, we were on our way, airborne and heading north, sweat and all. With all the long and difficult attempts to get in the air, the engine temperature had climbed to the limit and I was quite relieved to see it drop a few degrees. Continued overworking of the engine could raise cane with the engine and possibly cause it to burn out. This is always a bush pilot's concern when carrying big loads. It limits the capacity of the performance of an airplane in so many cases.

It was always interesting that when I passed over Sunapee Harbor where my mother worked at a gift shop, she would recognize the heavy drone of my airplane engine when I was flying north. She would rush out in the parking lot and wave to me wishing me a good and safe trip. And in turn, I would wave my wings to say, "see you later mom."

Flying so far north, and my being gone for a week at a time, gave her some concern. She was always asking me," can't you find some other kind of profession that is safer? You're always doing something crazy and dangerous to get yourself killed." I would tell her, "mom, there just wouldn't be any fun doing it, if there wasn't a challenge to it."

A STORM'S
FURY UNLEASHES

My life as a bush pilot seemed to fill my needs, but to me, it was a joy to bring adventure to those that I fly and to see the smile on their faces in their successes in hunting and fishing.

As we continued our flight north over the rolling hills and mountains of New Hampshire, we enjoyed the sight of scattered beaver dams tucked away on the side hills with their glittering waters reflecting in the bright sunlight. I often thought as I passed over these beaver dams how I would like to take the time to hike in to where they were to maybe catch a few tasty native brook trout. Of course, they wouldn't stack up to the kind of trout we catch in northern Canada.

Along the Connecticut River valley bordering Vermont and New Hampshire stood the many sharp corn stocks from the farmer's fresh cutting of corn. Field after field of all designs lay along the valley. Some freshly plowed and some still laden with six to eight foot corn stocks still with their ears of corn hanging, ready to be picked.

We could see the farmers busy at work cleaning up their hay fields and hauling the corn silage to the barns. How fortunate for the farmers to have miles and miles of such rich soil in the Connecticut River valley.

Flying at lower altitudes allows us to appreciate more of what 'Mother Nature" provides for us. Seeing wild game throughout the hillsides and the many wild fowl such as geese and ducks along the lakes and ponds makes our trip more interesting.

Stopping to clear Canadian Customs at a small pier on Memphremagog Lake was a must to keep us out of trouble with the Canadian officials. If a pilot, or his passengers get caught doing something wrong inside Canada, he stands a very good chance of having his airplane seized. I never felt I had the extra money to spend on a lawyer, so figured it was best to behave myself and make sure the fellows with me did the same.

Lake Memphremagog can be one heck of a rough lake when the wind gets kicking up a storm. Any huge lake gives the wind plenty of chances to build up some wicked beg waves by the time it blows from the north end to the south end. At times, it seemed like I was landing my seaplane in the middle of an ocean when I landed on this particular lake. The only way I could save from dealing with such huge waves was to land as close to the shore as possible taking advantage of the trees to help break the wind.

It was another story when taking off. The seaplane would porpoise so badly at times, I thought I would go for the deep six, airplane and all. Knowing my seaplane and its capabilities was a big help. I knew with a given load, just how much I could ask of my seaplane in about any kind of condition. Most importantly, it was up to me to keep my passengers safe.

It also was a good practice to take advantage of the winds aloft to make better time. Sometimes the wind would be blowing stronger at a certain higher altitude, and sometimes it would be to my advantage to fly at a lower altitude. Whatever the case may be, it is better to fly with a tailwind which will increase your ground speed.

Bucking headwinds not only can slow an airplane down considerably, but it uses a lot more fuel on a given trip. That spells "money," that can be used for a

A STORM'S
FURY UNLEASHES

much better purpose. If I am flying north on a sunny day, you can almost be assured of a headwind, unless it is the day before a storm. In that case, the wind is apt to be coming from the south giving me a nice tailwind.

As we fly in a northeasterly direction along the St. Lawrence River, we pass by Quebec City arriving by the mouth of the Saguenay River that flows out of Lac St. Jean. At this point of the trip we start seeing a lot of white whales that congregate around the edge of where the fresh water meets the brackish seawater.

One of the spectacular sights to see are the black humpback whales when they surface like a submarine and blowing a huge spout of water. As I flew low over the sandbars, we could see hundreds of seals laying on the sand sunning themselves, enjoying the warm sun.

Baie Comeau was our next stop. Labrador Air Safari, a seaplane base located a mile or two up the Manicougan River is our jumping off place before heading north to a set of camps on the headwaters of the Caniapiscau River that I enjoyed for quite a few years. This would be the last place to refuel before arriving at the camps.

It was always a problem with a full load of fuel to climb to a high enough altitude to clear the power lines stretched across the river. Dodging pulpwood that floated in the river was another problem.

One of the pilots flying in the area had hit a piece of pulpwood on landing and drove it through the front of his floats. Just one more thing for a bush pilot to look out for, when landing on rivers where logging operations are taking place.

A STORM'S
FURY UNLEASHES

Flying north following the Manicougan River was an interesting trip. Black bear, moose and watching fish rising to the top of rivers and lakes kept our interest along the way. It was about two and one half-hours to camp and the further north we flew the more anxious we got to sink a line in one of the rivers.

Watching the big change in the environment as we flew north was like flying from one world into another, to a world that is totally different. It was like stepping from civilization into the wilds of the unknown. The further north we flew, the more lakes and rivers we could see in all directions.

When I look at my flight maps of northern Canada, about all I can see is blue indicating water just about everywhere. It seems so unbelievable that there can be so much water surrounded by nothing but barren lands. And yet, there is so much wild life in the North Country. I guess that is why it is so intriguing to me each time I fly north.

I had flown this route so many times I could fly it in my sleep, but when the camps came into sight, it always gave me a special feeling of being someplace special. A place to relax without the phone ringing and nobody to bug me. I knew once I got my fishing rod out and made a few casts in the river, I would be in my glory.

By the time we get to camp it is usually late in the day, just in time for a good meal, make plans for the next day, and hit the sack for some good rest after a long day of flying.

The following day had brought a few surprises. The sky appeared to be threatening with very dark clouds indicating we may be getting some severe thunder-

A STORM'S
FURY UNLEASHES

storms. My partner had flown some of his group to a river east of the camps, but failed to advise me as to the location as to where he dropped them off. After leaving them on their own on the river, he flew into Labrador City to get some supplies. Well, I guess that didn't set too well with me.

First off, I don't ever like the idea of dropping someone off back in the wilderness, especially without survival gear, a tent and sleeping bags, and some food. By mid-afternoon, the weather had deteriorated to the point where I had become quite concerned about the safety of my partner, as well as the fellows he flew off to another river.

The sky had let loose with the fiercest of storms I had witnessed in a long time. It looked more like tornado weather than anything. Bolts of lightning lit up the skies like the celebration of the fourth of July with all the fireworks. Between the wicked loud booms of thunder and hailstones as big as golf balls bouncing off the ground, it reminded me of some of the storms they have out in the mid-west.

It was getting late in the day, and still no sign of my partner and his friends. Nobody in his right mind should be flying in this kind of weather. It would be just plain suicide to stick your neck out and think you could survive very long flying through a storm with this magnitude.

My son asks, "dad, don't you think we should go and look for them, what if something has happened?" For fear that maybe the people are in big trouble I did what no pilot should have done. Having no idea as to the exact location or whereabouts of my partner and his friends, the thought of risking my neck to rescue

A STORM'S
FURY UNLEASHES

them became the only thing to do. It had become apparent that something must be wrong and the quicker I could find them, the better.

Looking across the lake and seeing huge waves whipping down the lake due to the high winds wasn't exactly appealing to me, but time was of the essence. It was either leave now, or it would be too late to fly before darkness overtook us.

My son Richard climbed into the co-pilot seat next to me to act as a second set of eyes to help locate our missing people. There was little question that we were going to be in for a rough ride. With the sky black as a boot from the dark clouds above and the gusty winds accompanied by updrafts and downdrafts, it gave me a hassle and a half trying to get in the air.

Visibility was down to a minimum due to the heavy rain and fog making it almost impossible to see where to fly. Trying to map read was unbelievably difficult flying in such conditions and at treetop level. I couldn't always fly in a straight line in the direction I wanted to go due to the poor visibility and the hills, so I was forced to detour in several places and hoped I could find my way through the storm.

Lightning bolts were striking all around the airplane with the sudden clash of thunder echoing through the fuselage like someone striking a giant base drum in our ears. The airplane was being tossed about like a toy bottle in the middle of an ocean and any moment I was expecting the storm to drive us into a side hill.

As much as I needed my son's help to watch out for treetops and rivers where the people may be, I wished I hadn't put his life at risk. Flying from one river or lake to another, circling about in a desperate

A STORM'S
FURY UNLEASHES

search for people I had no idea where they might be, seemed so ridiculous, but I felt as though I couldn't give up. Somewhere out there, were four people and an airplane, but the big question was where.

I tried reaching them by radio with no response. Flying conditions weren't getting any better, and the thought of getting forced down in this kind of weather didn't make me any happier. The mere fact that we were able to stay in the air was a miracle in itself. I half expected that at any moment to get knocked out of the air by a bolt of lightning, then we really would have been in trouble.

My hands became stiff and callused from hanging on to the controls for such a long period of time in such rough conditions. As the time ticked by I decided to try one last place on a river a little north of where we had been searching. It was a case of having to be directly over the ones we were looking for in order to see them with all the rain and fog.

As I made a low pass at a bend in the river, I could make out three people waving frantically for help. It was a touch and go situation trying to land in such a difficult condition, but I managed to pull up to where the three were. When I got out of my seaplane, I was staring at what appeared to be three drenched men, totally soaked to the hide, and scared to death. They thought they had been abandoned and left to die.

I was told their pilot had dropped them off with no food, tent, or sleeping bags and had flown to Labrador City with no idea when he may be back. This was bad news as I stated earlier, this just should not have been done. To leave someone stranded out in the bush with no survival gear is definitely a no-no.

A STORM'S
FURY UNLEASHES

The three drenched men didn't waste much time climbing aboard my seaplane, but how we would be able to make it safely back to camp was the next thing. I would have to use all of my experience and then some to get us there. There was no letup of the storm, and getting all of us killed wasn't a good idea.

The visibility was so bad it was all I could do to see good enough to miss hitting the trees overhanging the riverbank while flying off the river. The three men were so happy to have been rescued they could care less how dangerous the flying was. When the bolts of lightning illuminated the inside of the airplane, their faces showed little or no sign of concern. I told myself, "these guys don't really understand the dangers of flying in a storm of this magnitude."

The added weight in the airplane put more stress on the wings and every time a strong gust of wind hit us I thought the wings were going to be torn off. I had never flown in such a storm in all my years as a pilot. My son Richard was having his first real experience first hand at what it was like to fly in such bad weather. Yet, he seemed to be cool, calm, and collected.

I was happy that he was sitting beside me to help out watching for the hills that I had to dodge in all the poor visibility and heavy rain. Every time a bolt of lightning would come flashing by the airplane, Richard would say, "Wow, that was close, I sure hope we can make it back to camp soon."

That sixty miles or so back to camp seemed more like an eternity. At any moment I expected to get blown out of the sky. Had I not known some of the area we were flying in, it would have been a lot tougher. When the camps finally came in sight, it was a

A STORM'S
FURY UNLEASHES

great relief for everyone. The next thing was to land the seaplane safely in a spot next to the camps where the huge waves weren't buffeting the shoreline so much. To cause a crash so close to the camps would be a catastrophe and a half. After landing and securing the seaplane I felt like kissing the ground, and by the looks on the faces of everyone else, I think they felt the same. Maybe someday, I will learn to say "no," about when to fly. No wonder I got bald at an early age.

During the night the storm had finally subsided, and as the early morn dawned, what a beautiful surprise to see a bright light on the horizon in the east, called the sun.

As I looked out across the lake from the camp, a calm mirror like surface on the water glistened as the sun's rays flickered in the few patches of light fog rising from the lake. I could hear the loons calling from different parts of the lake signaling to each other, "come on over and join us for breakfast." The loon is such a majestic bird to watch when they do their mating dance on the water.

There was all heck to pay when the heavy drone of a Cessna approached the camp that morning. Our friend's pilot was returning from Labrador City. The damage had been done, and the only thing left to do was to read him the right-act about leaving someone stranded out in the boonies.

The three men voiced their opinion as well, and needless to say, were not in a joking mood. I can only add, that it is so very important that a pilot use more common sense in making his decisions. It might save someone a lot of grief.

A STORM'S
FURY UNLEASHES

As the mountains cleared of fog and the sun burned away the remaining moisture from the storm of the day before, I began making plans to enjoy a day or two of fishing with my son. My wife would accompany us along with my son's friends.

We could breath easy for the rest of the day, as there was no storm in sight, so following through with my plans of flying out to a remote river was of no concern. With the task of packing a lunch and getting our fishing gear organized and loaded into the seaplane, our anxiety began to build.

Questions started racing through our minds. " Have those huge trophy brook trout made their way from the deep holes in the lakes into the rapids of the river to do their spawning?" "Gee, I wonder if the trout are going to be fasting, and not bite at all?" "We have come all this way and the fishing is going to be lousy."

Flying to one of my hotspots for fishing brought all of our concerns to an end. With each cast, a beautiful speckled brook trout fell victim to a net. Trout ranging from three to eight and nine pounds racing from one end of the rapids to another to throw the hook that held them captive on the end of a fly line or spinning line. Throughout the day, as we explored other sections of the river, time, and time again, the same kind of success repeated itself over and over.

It was as though the trout knew we were coming to fish that day, and they were going to give us a treat of a lifetime. I have to say, "they kept their word on that one." An amateur fisherman couldn't make a mistake on this particular day. No matter where we cast our lines, a trout was there to grab it. This was a day of fishing we would all remember for years to come.

A STORM'S
FURY UNLEASHES

From time to time, the thrill of hooking on to a large salmon or lake trout added a little extra fun to our fishing. It was apparent that we hit a prime time for our fishing trip with the exception of the worst weather we had ever experienced the day before.

For the next couple of days, we enjoyed some of the finest weather. My son and his friends found out what it was like to hook onto some large northern pike. They broke more lines and lost more lures trying to land the fish. Once a northern pike decides to leave the territory, forget it. When they grab your line, they swallow it up about a foot and a half and their sharp teeth cut the line like a knife cutting through butter.

The fun of having a seaplane and a well seasoned bush pilot with you makes all the difference in the world whether you enjoy your trip or not. It's so nice to be able to jump in the seaplane and head out to some remote area to wet a line or two.

Just the feeling of having nobody around besides your own group is relaxing enough. Another thing is, you don't have to worry about someone's fishing line wrapping around your neck or hooking you behind the ear. That can be a little disturbing.

As the end of the week draws to a close, and the airplane is being loaded for the return trip home, the fond memories of the week of excellent fishing flashes through our mind. Thoughts of the many beautiful trophy brook trout that we caught and released. And let's not forget the storm that unleashed its wrath with such fury. There is always a new adventure to tell about when flying north.

My last days
As a bush pilot

Something tells me my last days as a bush pilot are drawing near. To have to give up living the life of a bush pilot for so many years as I have is already starting to work on my mind. It says, "Richard, you had better get cracking and do everything you have wanted to do as far as flying is concerned before it is too late."

Somehow, it saddens me to think I would have to give up the freedom of flying around the North Country and Alaska in a 206 Cessna on floats. Perhaps I am being a little greedy asking for more years of flying, considering the many years that I have flown as a bush pilot and getting to meet thousands of clients.

If only I could get through a night's sleep without dreaming of flying a 206 Cessna on floats around the world. Maybe it's my past catching up to me with all the bad weather flying I have done. But maybe it's the nice days that I flew that's telling me, "Richard, wasn't it really nice flying when old "Mother Nature" gave you those nice sunny days and little wind, where you just leaned back in your seat and relaxed and did your thing?"

The only thing I can say to that is, "give me a new 206 Cessna and my health back and see what I do with it." It is so disturbing to have so many dreams about flying, when now I don't have my own airplane to fly. Renting an airplane doesn't do it for me, I want my own 206. Do you get the point?

MY LAST DAYS
AS A BUSH PILOT

Owning an airplane today is very expensive. The cost of insurance and maintenance has gotten out of reach for the average person, but when flying is in a person's blood, there's no stopping him from flying. He usually will find a way to satisfy his thirst.

Years ago, it was my thirst to become a bush pilot. Once I got the taste of what it was like to fly an airplane high in the sky to look down over the mountains and valleys, I knew then, that it would not be my last flight. Each flight I took only added to my thirst to fly more. It was like a driving force within me to do what I had dreamt of doing so many years past as a young boy.

From the very first day of taking my first flying lesson, to four days later when I soloed at six hours and ten minutes, the local pilots kept telling me that I was pushing things a little too quick. That I should slow down and take the time to absorb what I was learning. Who but me, knew what my capabilities were and perhaps my desire to fly was so great that nothing could stand in my way.

Getting my pilot's license in a couple of months and purchasing my first 206 Cessna with only a total of twenty-five hours was no small fete. As each day passed, the urge to fly to the North Country became stronger and stronger. My airplane was no good for what I wanted to use it for without a set of floats so after a second trip to the bank to get more money to buy the floats with, I was well on my way to heading north.

The same day I finished installing the floats on my 206 Cessna, I flew down to the Merrimack River by Hooksett, N.H. and got my seaplane rating. I was so

MY LAST DAYS
AS A BUSH PILOT

happy to have achieved all this in such a short time, I couldn't wait to fly back to Lake Sunapee to get my fishing gear and survival equipment and head eighteen hundred miles north to Hudson Bay in northern Quebec.

From then on I joined the ranks of the elite bush pilots up north. One of the problems I encountered while flying in the Province of Quebec was the language barrier. Some of the pilots only spoke French, so I kind of had to fake it a bit with what little French I knew.

Times that I was forced to land near a village because of bad weather, a good share of the people that showed their hospitality to me and my friends spoke mostly French. I found myself having to learn some of the French language in difficult situations. When I shrugged my shoulders during certain conversations with French speaking people, it usually was a sign that I didn't understand what they were saying.

The people in Quebec didn't mind listening to my attempts to speak French as much as they didn't feel comfortable about speaking English to me. They seem to be afraid of making a mistake. At times, I am sure it was amusing to all of us.

Though my life as a bush pilot brought me fame, it didn't bring me fortune in the money sense. In another sense, my fortune was in the form of enjoying what I liked to do best. Flying to remote areas fishing and hunting, and most of all, enjoying what "Mother Nature" provided us. Eating off the lands of the wilds, such as wild cranberries, blueberries, raspberries, deer, moose, and caribou. We must not forget the tasty brook trout or the walleye pike cooked to a nice

MY LAST DAYS
AS A BUSH PILOT

delicious golden brown in deep butter over an open fire.

How many times did a mink and all his cousins sneak up onto a rock beside me and steal away with some of the finest brook trout I could catch. I would be standing on the shore of a river casting out for one of those fine trophy speckled brook trout and several otter would swim up to me. The next thing to happen, they would stick their heads out of the water, whistle to me, and with a swish of their tail, disappear, only to come back for another look later.

To me, just the joy of being in the North Country is reward enough. Once I cross the Canadian border and on my way north, I leave behind me all the frustrations of dealing with things I have no control over.

My thoughts are only of the enjoyment of flying from one lake to another exploring new fishing holes, or to a remote river loaded with beautiful brook trout. To watch the majestic trophy bull caribou prancing over the wide-open hills with his antlers thrown back over his shoulders.

Speaking of caribou, I may as well tell you about the time that I took a couple of friends of mine up in the North Country to hunt caribou. The trip originated from Lake Sunapee, New Hampshire flying my usual route by way of Memphremagog Lake at Newport, Vermont, past Sherbrooke and Quebec City, and on to the St. Lawrence River to Baie Comeau. From there we flew up the Manicouagan River to the camp on the headwaters of the Caniapiscau River.

A good nights rest and a hearty meal the following morning put us in good spirits before departing to a place I had hunted caribou north of Chefferville. Being

MY LAST DAYS
AS A BUSH PILOT

sometime the latter part of September brought a mixture of bad weather. Rain in the lower elevations, and snow in the higher mountains. It seemed that every time I wanted to fly further up in the North Country it stormed and this was no exception.

Most of the higher mountains were in clouds hidden from view. Whenever I tried ducking through a notch in the mountains a snowstorm would move in to block it. Most of the mountains were running north and south and gave few places to fly through. I either had to take my chances and grab the first opportunity that came and make my way through a notch to get on the other side. Once I was able to do that, I had another row of mountains to contend with.

Whatever the case was, it kept me on my toes, busy map reading and watching my compass. I didn't have a GPS (Global positioning instrument) to tell me exactly where I was. I have always flown by the seat of my britches and my maps when flying in northern Canada. I find that navigating in this manner gets me to where I want to go safely and by using the maps, I can tell where the lakes and rivers are in case I have to make a quick decision to land.

In today's world, more pilots are using the GPS instruments successfully. I always ask, "what if the GPS fails, what do you do then?" If a pilot isn't able to map read well, he is in big trouble, especially in the North Country.

His only other alternative is to fly by the aid of the sun, but what if the sun isn't shining on that particular day. Then he had better get out his paddle and paddle his seaplane down some river that eventually might get him out to civilization.

MY LAST DAYS
AS A BUSH PILOT

Getting back to my caribou hunting story, the only way I could get to our destination was to fly through the lower valleys jumping from one lake or river to the next. The last mountain range to cross beyond the Caniapiscau River and to the east was socked in solid with snowstorms. Flying such a distance and being so close to where I wanted to hunt made me more determined than ever.

I knew of a river further north that wound its way through the mountain that I was having a hard time to cross. It just might let us sneak down that so we could make it to my special spot for hunting.

It was never what I call fun fighting snowstorms, rain and fog, flying through and around mountains that could take your life in a whisper. But what is bush flying about? I couldn't just sit at the camp all the time and wait for the good days. My friends and I wouldn't get anywhere, nor have the success that we so often enjoy.

When we finally got to our destination, I landed the seaplane on a long, narrow lake. On the eastside of the lake a small river flowed out through a maze of tangled alders and stunted spruce trees from the many years of severe winters. The caribou had managed to wind their way through this swampy low land leaving trails in all directions.

Depending on how late in the season the warm weather prevailed decided when the caribou would start their migration. From the middle of summer on there is always a few stragglers that wander here and there that makes hunting them more fun, at least to me. But when the migration really gets under way, there are thousands of caribou that gather from all

MY LAST DAYS
AS A BUSH PILOT

over north and central Labrador and make their way to northwestern Quebec in the vicinity of Hudson Bay.

To witness such a migration of caribou is an unbelievable sight. Thousands of caribou are lying around the hills waiting for more to join up with them to make their mass move. But you have to be there at the right time when all this happens.

As we made our way along the river that wound its way through the swamp we could see an occasional caribou picking its way around the trees. Some with huge antlers and others just what I call average. The sportsmen usually like to shoot the trophy caribou for their antlers, but the Indians and Eskimos like to shoot the female caribou for better eating. The female caribou have antlers as well, but are much smaller and shaped different than the male.

One of the hunters decided to shoot an old bull that had antlers about five feet wide. The woods were so thick it was difficult to see a lot of caribou at any given time, so we decided to head back to the seaplane. It seemed that while we were in the swamp poking around looking for caribou, they were out on the edge of the lake walking the beach right under the tail section of my seaplane. I guess it was easier walking for them.

When the fellows saw all the tracks on the beach, they wished they had stayed by the seaplane. They wouldn't have had to work so hard carrying the meat out of the woods. We knew the caribou were on the move, but just how much we couldn't tell for sure. Because of the bad weather floating around and getting late in the day, we decided it was best to head back to camp. We could come back in a day or two.

MY LAST DAYS
AS A BUSH PILOT

Two days had passed before we were able to return to the same place. The only problem, nothing looked the same. Something had happened that completely changed the landscape forever. A mass migration of caribou by the thousands had moved through the area that we had been just two days before.

It was like an army of bulldozers had gone to work and bulldozed every spruce tree and alder bush into the ground completely leveling the swampy area into one huge mudflat. If I hadn't seen this with my own eyes, I would not have believed it was possible. There was not a caribou in sight anywhere. How could so many caribou move through an area in such a short time and completely disappear I will never know. I guess I could say it was an act of nature.

Here again, it was a good thing I had my own seaplane. I knew where the caribou were headed and it was up to me to catch up to the herd. Being outdone by caribou was not my idea of success. We jumped in the 206 and headed northwest up in no-man's land.

With extra fuel on board we were able to fly beyond the normal range of the 206 Cessna and not have to worry about enough fuel to get us back to camp. The area we were flying to, is barren territory with the exception of a few trees along some of the lake shores and rivers.

It gives a person the feeling that he is in another world, desolate and abandoned except for the few birds and animals that dare brave the severe conditions in the North Country.

Once the caribou have made up their mind to migrate north, it's like they are on a time clock schedule. Night and day, they move steadily to their winter quar-

MY LAST DAYS
AS A BUSH PILOT

ters. But even when they finally reach their destination, they don't stay there very long. They soon begin their move back to the southeast. It's like they are on the move continuously. Maybe that's the way "Mother Nature" has worked out their food supply situation.

Because of the huge caribou population and the long period of time to grow lichen, their primary diet, it is better that they stay on the move. This way, they won't eat up all the food in one area.

For a while, I thought the caribou had sprouted wings. It was quite a while before we finally caught up to the tail end of the herd. Even then, it was difficult to distinguish the difference between a caribou and the moss on the ground. The colors of the caribou are such that it gives them good camouflage making them hard to detect.

There was little problem finding a lake to land on that gave us some advantage for hunting, for everywhere we looked there was water. In a short time and with the use of binoculars it was fairly easy choosing a trophy caribou to fill our tags. We didn't have to chase over the mountains after caribou like I have in the past. We could sit and wait for one to come along.

The big problem of dressing the animals began and the job of skinning the trophy caribou heads so the hunters could have a cape for mounting. As a rule, if we fly several hundred miles north of the camp, we end up camping out over night. By the time we get our caribou it is usually too late to make the flight back to camp before dark.

Flying after dark in the North Country with a seaplane isn't the best of practices. With all the thousands of lakes, it's hard to map read when I am look-

MY LAST DAYS
AS A BUSH PILOT

ing down into nothing but darkness. It's nice to be able to make out the outline of the lakes in order to compare with what I am looking at on my flight maps.

There are too many rocks sticking up near the surface of the lakes to take a chance landing, especially if I am not that familiar with them. As it is, I figure I have been lucky to survive as many years as I have. Not only that, but there are too many snowstorms that time of year to stick my neck out too far. It's bad enough flying during daylight hours.

I am fortunate to have enjoyed so many years as a bush pilot, and I am sure that most of the people I have flown have enjoyed their trips, either for hunting or fishing.

The summer season being so short, in the month of August the nights start cooling down in a hurry. It is not unusual to have the temperatures in the twenties. The water temperature in the lakes and rivers drop considerably because of the cool nights and by the time the first of September rolls around, it's time for old man winter to start doing his thing.

In the north we have two seasons, a real short summer, and a long winter. It doesn't give the animals much of a chance to get acclimated to the warmer weather. It seems like the geese no sooner have their young and the mother and dad are pushing them to learn how to fly so they can head south. The geese seem to show a great devotion towards their young.

I really enjoy watching the snow geese and the Canadian geese watching over their little ones waddling around doing the goose step. The mother and dad occasionally have a hard time guarding their young against attacks from wolves. Several times I

MY LAST DAYS
AS A BUSH PILOT

have witnessed seeing the wolves chasing after the geese, big and small, grabbing them by the wing or neck and take off with them.

About the time the blueberries are ready to eat, the snow starts coming. That's when we see thousands of geese along the hillsides feeding on the blueberries storing up energy before flying south. From that point on, it's a case of survival of the fittest. The weak ones can't make the flight and are left behind to fall prey to the wolves or an arctic fox.

One of the interesting kinds of birds that live in the far north is the ptarmigan, a grouse of mountainous and northern cold regions. During the summer it is mostly brown with a white chest, and in the winter it changes its color to all white, camouflaging it totally against the snow-white background.

Quite often, while we are caribou hunting, and as it happens, just as we are about shoot a caribou, a flock of ptarmigan will come from nearby bushes, start making their clucking noises "cluck cluck, cluck cluck," and then all take off with a big fluttering noise, upsetting our hunt.

I used to chase them around the hillsides with my hunting knife trying to catch one for a good hot meal, but found them to be very illusive. I spent more time looking for my knife than what it was worth. Little things like this, is what helps make my flying north interesting and enjoyable.

On one of my caribou hunting trips, I was taxiing the seaplane out in the middle of a lake next to a big bull caribou. One of my hunter friends says, "Richard, I'll bet you twenty-five dollars you can't ride one of those caribou." When I climbed onto the top of the

MY LAST DAYS
AS A BUSH PILOT

floats and stuck my hand into the ice cold water, I quickly called the bet off. No way was I jumping into that lake to ride the caribou. I would have been frozen solid. The guys are always trying something for a kick or two.

Late in the caribou season it is unusual to have two nice days in a row. After flying north of the camps and having a successful hunt, the task of getting back to camp gets pretty rough sometimes. What's worse, later in the day, conditions deteriorate.

When the government of Quebec decided to flood a big share of the North Country for hydroelectric power, it left nothing but treetops sticking up out of the dammed up area. It seemed weird seeing all the spruce treetops in a body of water that is hundreds of square miles.

The weather had gotten so bad I was forced to fly water level over every lake or river I could follow. It was tough flying through all the snowstorms, rain and fog. As the end of day neared, and we were only thirty minutes from camp, the visibility got so poor I had to land in the middle of the huge dammed up body of water.

The only place I could find to tie up the seaplane was a spruce treetop that stuck out of the water about two feet. The visibility was so poor I couldn't see where to taxi or see the shoreline of the lake. We had no choice but to take all the caribou meat out of the seaplane and lay along the deck of the floats to make room for all of us to sleep.

Talk about roughing it, with stinky feet from head to feet and trying to get a night's sleep was almost impossible. We had to rap ourselves in our sleeping

MY LAST DAYS
AS A BUSH PILOT

bags and hope for the best. Needless to say, it was a long night. With all the water around us we didn't have to worry about the wolves getting their teeth into our caribou. Normally, I let the guys use my tent while I sleep on a foam mattress in the airplane. I find it hard to compete with them when they snored so loud.

The only problem, we didn't have any dry ground around us to pitch the tent. It's a good thing I don't get seasick on fresh water, only in the ocean.

After a long and uneasy night I peered out the window into a grey mass of fog. It was so thick I could barely make out the caribou quarters lined along the floats. The only thing to do was to lay back down and draw my sleeping back a little closer around my head and wait for the fog to would lift, hopefully for not too many hours.

It was a good thing I don't sleepwalk, I would have walked off the floats into the water. Every time I fly guys north, I tell them don't be surprised if we have to rough it a bit, but there is a limit as to how much you want to put up with. This little ordeal took all the joy out of what was a real hunting adventure.

It wasn't until midmorning before I was able to see land and have the visibility good enough to fly. At least the caribou meat got a good chilling being exposed to the cold night air. The rest of the trip back to camp went off without a hitch with the exception of dodging a few patches of fog.

We didn't waste much time at camp getting the 206 refueled and checked out for the return trip home. My friends had filled their tags and after such an ordeal were anxious to head home. One thing that was usually in my favor, was the fact that the further south I flew, the milder the temperature, and the better the weather.

You would think that as many trips that I have flown from New Hampshire to northern Canada it would become "old hat," but every trip had its own adventure and something new. Sure, the people were different, but the new faces brought something new to the trip as well. Each trip brought a new challenge. One thing that was guaranteed, we never knew what was in store for us.

My years as a bush pilot were drawing to an end. The man upstairs was beginning to whisper in my ear that I had had enough of this kind of flying and it was close to the time for me to start thinking about packing it in.

Though my interest and flying spirit was running on high, circumstances and finances began to take its toll. It was like a sickening feeling inside me that I was going to have to give up living the life as a bush pilot like I had been doing all these years.

I figured, if only I could get in another season, maybe I could enjoy a few more thrills and adventure that might outdo some of the wild challenges that confronted me in the past. Not that I was out to get myself killed, but I just wanted to go out in a little bit of glory, if you know what I mean.

Yes, there would be a few more fishing and hunting trips. And there would be a few more trophy speckled brook trout with my name on them. My 206 Cessna was still in top shape and had served me well. The engine had been overhauled recently which meant I could fly through the season without any great expense.

MY LAST DAYS
AS A BUSH PILOT

My ears were so tuned in to the sound of the engine, that the slightest problem that may develop I could detect way in advance. I guess that comes from flying the same type aircraft for so many years.

Early spring in northern Canada is not the same as early spring in New England. We may consider early spring to be in March and April, but in northern Canada it is not until June. The ice usually doesn't go out of the lakes until the middle of June.

Fishing for lake trout in June right after the ice goes out of the lakes is terrific. Almost every tributary to the lakes are loaded with lake trout. Because the lakes are usually so large, I find it easier to hop in the 206 and fly around to the different streams, rather than take a boat from camp.

It's common to catch twelve and fourteen-pound lake trout, but quite often we hook into some in the thirty to forty pound range. When we get one of the big ones on, they head for the bottom of the lake and sit there. With a lot of tugging on the line, they finally take off for another part of the lake. That's when you have your hands full trying to reel them in.

When the water is really high in the streams from the melting snows, I have caught lake trout weighing up to forty plus pounds and about fifty inches long. The lake trout are in the rivers feeding on brook trout, and whatever else they can get their jaws on.

Because of their size, the smaller brook trout hang out in the faster water to avoid the lake trout and northern pike. When summer comes and the water starts warming up, "what did I say," it is rare that the water gets warm enough to stick your toes in without freezing them off.

MY LAST DAYS
AS A BUSH PILOT

The month of July gives a variation of fishing where a person is apt to catch just about anything that frequents the rivers and lakes. Of course, it helps to know what you are doing and the right kind of lure or bait to use. Then comes August, it is the prime month for catching that long sought after beautiful trophy brook trout.

"Mother Nature" has signaled the brook trout that lie deep in the holes of the lakes it's time to head for the rivers and rapids to do their spawning. Once in the river, the female will begin her search for a spot that has a gravel bottom to lay her eggs. She only has a certain time to do her thing before she has to head back into the protection of the big lakes before winter.

Then along comes the male trout to pair up with the female to fertilize the eggs by spilling its sperm over the eggs and begins to fan the water with its tail to help scatter the sperm among the eggs. It's all part of a cycle to keep the generation continuing.

It is a beautiful sight to see the trout doing their spawning act as my friends and I would stand on the edge of a pool where the river makes a bend providing a calmer area for the trout. Seeing such trophy brook trout laying practically still, finning in the clear pristine waters of the north gives me great pleasure. And then, to see how quick they are to rise to the surface to take a fly that comes drifting by.

I know you have read earlier in the book how my friends and I have had the fun of a lifetime catching the huge brookies, but to tell you one last time, there is nothing like hooking onto one of these trout. So red in the bellies and so pretty the red and blue spots on their sides. When I see one these trout rise to the sur-

MY LAST DAYS
AS A BUSH PILOT

face and flash its big square tail in the air I can expect a good fight.

If someone were to ask me, "What would I like to do if I had my life to live all over again?" I would have to tell them I would like to relive my life as a bush pilot, only do more of it, if that's possible. I guess I was born to live the adventures in the wilds among the fruits of "Mother Nature," to meet the challenges of the north and fly with the freedom of the eagles, to soar over the mountains and lakes to enjoy its beauty.

I will miss flying my 206 Cessna that has given me so much joy. Perhaps in the spirit of my dreams I can continue the life I loved so much. Who knows what another day will bring? For those that read my stories, I wish them the best. Happy dreams, and maybe someday, you too will enjoy an adventure in your life similar to what I have. I am sure that one day I will be flying on the wings of an angel.

PREVIOUS BOOKS
WRITTEN BY AUTHOR

THE ADVENTURES OF
A BUSH PILOT
FIRST PRINTING: 1997

.......is a series of short stories about the life of a bold and daring bush pilot that flew against the challenges of the North. It begins with the hazards of his younger days and growing up to realize his boyhood dreams of wanting to fly. It takes you briefly through some of his childhood experiences to give you an idea of what shaped his character and how he learned to fly.

It tells about the problems of getting his first airplane and becoming a bush pilot and guide. How he takes on the challenges of flying sportsmen in Alaska salmon fishing and his close encounters with grizzlies. Read about the wild adventures of hunting caribou and moose in northern Canada, and how he managed to deal with "Mother Nature" in coping with the severe weather conditions that exists in the far north. Learn about his successes in fishing for salmon and the trophy speckled brook trout. More importantly, how he gave of himself in rescuing lost hunters and occupants of downed aircraft.